Love Reading

ALISON DAVID

EGMONT

EGMONT

We bring stories to life

*For Louis and Ibe,
you are both my inspiration.*

*For Mum,
for starting me on the reading journey.*

First published in Great Britain in 2014 by Egmont UK Limited
The Yellow Building, 1 Nicholas Road
London, W11 4AN

Text copyright © 2014 Alison David

The moral rights of the author have been asserted

ISBN 978 1 4052 7154 7

1 3 5 7 9 10 8 6 4 2

www.egmont.co.uk

A CIP catalogue record for this title is available from the British Library

Printed and bound in Great Britain by the CPI Group

57322/1

Stay safe online. Any website addresses listed in this book are correct at the time of going to print. However, Egmont is not responsible for content hosted by third parties. Please be aware that online content can be subject to change and websites can contain content that is unsuitable for children. We advise that all children are supervised when using the internet.

EGMONT

Our story began over a century ago, when seventeen-year-old Egmont Harald Petersen found a coin in the street. He was on his way to buy a flyswatter, a small hand-operated printing machine that he then set up in his tiny apartment.

The coin brought him such good luck that today Egmont has offices in over 30 countries around the world. And that lucky coin is still kept at the company's head offices in Denmark.

CONTENTS

Introduction 1

Chapter 1: Screen time: finding a balance 18

Chapter 2: Pre-school: ages 0–4 32

Chapter 3: Starting school: ages 5–7 56

Chapter 4: Choosing to read: ages 8–11 90

Chapter 5: Staying connected: ages 12–16 . . . 118

Bookshelf 152

Resources and acknowledgments 156

Introduction

EXPERT VIEW

Children who read for pleasure are not only better at English but are also better at maths. Children who read for pleasure make more progress over time. Reading for pleasure brings a wider vocabulary and enables the child to take on new concepts.

Dr Alice Sullivan, Institute of Education

I believe reading for pleasure is one of the greatest gifts a parent can give their child. It is a gift of love that will stay with them throughout their life. I am passionate about encouraging children to read for enjoyment. This is a book for parents who also want that for their child.

Everyone knows that reading is the foundation of learning and education, but what is less well known is that if a child reads for pleasure it is the single biggest indicator of their likely future success – much more than parents' educational background or social status (see page 72). It's also an amazing way for a mother or father to bond with their child. The magic of story and the shared experience of reading together in the early years will stay with you throughout their childhood and beyond.

I have learned a lot about helping children love reading

through being a mum and through my work. Louis, my son, is now a teenager and we have, in the course of his life so far, read hundreds of books together. I can honestly say that reading to and with him is one of the most joyful and pleasurable things we do together. I have seen Louis blossom, grow and flourish through the power of reading. I have spent a lot of time encouraging him – as well as my nephew and niece and the children of friends – to read.

I work for Egmont, a children's book and magazine publishing company, and my job involves researching and interviewing children and their parents to understand what encourages and what hinders reading. I want to know why and how children's reading thrives in some families, despite the myriad distractions of life, and why in some families it struggles. I also work with schools, seeking out teachers' opinions on how reading for pleasure can be encouraged at home and at school. I regularly go into a primary school both for my job and as a volunteer to listen to the children reading. From every viewpoint I see both the magic that reading for pleasure brings, and the huge gap left if children don't experience it.

So my reasons for writing this book are to share what I know about helping children to love reading for pleasure and to explain why it is so important that they do.

Before I explore some of the fundamentals of childhood reading, I have some questions for you to think about.

- **Do you consciously make sure there is some quiet time and that you have a routine for your child to read for pleasure?**
- **Do you regularly read to and with your child?**
- **Are all sorts of books and other reading materials, such**

as magazines, easily accessible and visible at home?
• Do you have rules limiting the amount of screen time your child can have?
• Does your child see you read for pleasure and do you make a point of having time away from screens?

If you answered no to any of these, read on! (And don't worry, you are not alone.)

How the book works

There is advice from the early years all the way through to the teens, so whatever age your child is when you come to this book you can find plenty of help and ideas. But to encourage a love of reading, the earlier you start the better. It allows the maximum time for your child to grow up with reading and for the love of it to take root and become part of their life.

Although the chapters are divided into age groups, they are guidelines only. I can't stress enough that all children are different, that they develop at different speeds and that there is no such thing as a typical child. So if your child is not yet at the reading stage I talk about, don't worry, don't get stressed, don't nag your child, just enjoy the special time you spend together reading. It will stick eventually.

Each chapter has advice on the reading habit, what the reading home should be like, how to read aloud and with your child, a list of handy Dos and Don'ts and some broad pointers to developmental stages in childhood appropriate to the age range. All of this is based on my research with families and schools, as well as my personal experiences. There are also comments from three specialists: David Reedy,

General Secretary of the United Kingdom Literacy Association and a literacy expert; Dr Amanda Gummer, a research psychologist and child development expert; and Dr Aric Sigman biologist and psychologist, who works on raising awareness among children, parents and doctors of the potential impact of electronic media and screen dependency.

Why is reading for pleasure vital?

This book is not about the academic importance of reading – there is little or no debate about that (or at least there shouldn't be). This book is about creating a lifelong love of reading for pleasure, because above all else there are so many wonderful things that reading brings to children: comfort and reassurance, confidence and security, relaxation, happiness and fun. It feeds their imagination, helps them to empathise and it even improves their sleeping patterns. And reading is a really important element of family life. It provides a connection between you and your child from the very early days through to teens and beyond. It's a strong 'glue' for your relationship, bringing you closer together through the sharing of reading and stories. It helps build long-lasting family ties and provides a shared set of stories and experiences that are unique to your family.

Without reading, childhood is poorer: children are missing out on one of life's great pleasures and the huge advantages that reading can bring. I talked with a teaching assistant who works with children who don't have happy lives – she sums up very well what reading can do:

> I work individually with the children who really struggle with reading. I spend extra time with them to support their learning and afterwards I often read to them. I will never forget one boy. He was 14 and a 'problem' child, always in trouble, aggressive, could barely read for himself and deprived in lots of ways. Over the weeks, I worked through the Alex Rider stories with him and he loved them. One day when I was reading aloud to him this troubled boy leaned over and rested his head on my shoulder. It made me so sad. We are not allowed to touch, much less hug the pupils, but he so needed it. It made me realise that reading is so much more than just the story.
>
> *Caroline, teaching assistant*

EXPERT VIEW

When children and young people are engaged in reading they learn crucially important lessons which will stand them in good stead throughout their lives. They learn that reading is fulfilling and that you do it for a variety of different purposes. Sometimes it is hard-going, but children develop the understanding that if they keep going they will achieve fulfilment and pleasure. This happens with all kinds of reading material, including novels, poems and information books.

David Reedy, literacy expert

You would think that with all these benefits reading would be really widespread. Yet, through my work and observations, I have seen children across the entire social scale who do not benefit from it and it truly makes me sad. I hope writing this book will help change things.

Why doesn't reading happen?

There are lots of reasons why children's reading is struggling. Its position, as a staple of entertainment and relaxation, has become challenged by hectic family lives and a simple lack of time; there has been too much emphasis placed on reading as a skill and not as a pleasure; and it has suffered in comparison to shiny new gadgets, devices and screen time in general.

Of course the age range covered in this book encompasses all of childhood so the demands and distractions vary hugely depending on the age of your child. In the pre-school years, you will have a lot more control over what your child gets up to. When school starts, the demands of after-school activities, clubs, homework and the wish to be with friends, will all impinge on the time you have together, and the time your child has separately, to read.

Meanwhile technology controls so much of the time available these days. Children of two won't be texting their friends (yet!), but they may well be playing games on a mobile phone. Teenagers will be texting their friends as well as playing games on their phone. Throughout the book I have provided age- or developmental-stage specific advice about how to free up time, regardless of the daily demands, to help your child enjoy reading.

One of the things that parents most often tell me is that they wish their child would read for pleasure, or read more than they do. Often they sound as if they think it's a lost cause. But it really is possible to change your family's and your child's habits. You just need to get involved to help make it happen.

The trouble is that we live in a very challenging world where time and energy are routinely sapped. As parents we are the ones who keep the show on the road, and we are under constant pressure as we try to juggle working life with home life, getting children up and to school, focusing attention on our work, their needs, meals and clean clothes, keeping the house in some semblance of order and supervising homework. Parents have told me they feel overwhelmed. The idea of making time each day for their child's reading, beyond schoolwork, seems like yet another thing to do.

Don't despair if this sounds like your life. The good news is it is not hard to find time for reading and it is absolutely not another chore. In fact it's a huge pleasure for you *and* your child. You will come to cherish the time you spend together.

> **EXPERT VIEW**
>
> Reading together can be a way of relaxing before bedtime and may promote more restful, easier sleep, so it's well worth the time spent. And children benefit hugely from having you to themselves for a period of time, even if it's just ten minutes.
>
> *Dr Amanda Gummer*

One of my recent research projects involved a very simple task for families with children at primary school. It was over a summer holiday and I asked parents to commit to at least ten minutes every day reading to or with their child. The results were amazing! In nearly every case the amount of reading and the enthusiasm for reading increased markedly. The response of Tariq (age 8) when he was back at school after the holidays was typical of the ones I got from just about all the children: 'I would like to read more and more each day. I love reading with my mum and dad.' One mum told me that before the project her daughter did not read for pleasure very much. Time was the main problem and the lack of a reading routine exacerbated it. The mother felt very guilty. After the holidays had ended, Rose (age 6) simply said 'I enjoyed it. I felt jolly and excited. When my mum finished reading I wanted her to read more.' This was on the back of simply setting aside ten minutes each day.

What you need to do

As you read through the book, you'll find lots of ideas and tips about how to read to and with your child, how to make your home a 'reading home' and so on. I just want to talk briefly about the fundamentals that underpin the whole 'project' of turning your child into a lifelong reader.

📖 Make a commitment

First you need to make a commitment to get involved and stay involved, probably for longer than you think. It is not a quick fix. You need to share with them and encourage them well into their teens, creating a rich environment for reading for pleasure to flourish.

📖 Avoid putting pressure on your child

The point about reading for pleasure is that it is for pleasure. Don't stress about the level your child is reading at or about the subject matter or format – the point is that they are reading. I've met many families where school reading becomes the priority. In the primary school years parents will talk about reading homework and focus on their child moving up the reading levels. I have also seen plenty of families where a bedtime story happens much less – or even not at all – because it is replaced by the child doing their school reading. Of course it's vital that our children learn to read. The world is competitive and they need to read to do well at school. But if we are not careful we can give them a message that reading is something they have to do, that it's a chore, that it's just homework. In their minds it can become no fun. If children feel pressured we can easily turn them off reading.

EXPERT VIEW

One of the best ways to take the pressure off is for them to see you enjoying reading and for you to talk to them about an interesting book you've read recently. Children learn by copying and you are your child's version of 'normal', so if you read for pleasure, they will expect to grow up reading too.

Dr Amanda Gummer

📖 Don't make assumptions

There is a prevailing assumption that once children can read, they will read. Not so! Quite simply, many children don't want to read because they don't associate it with pleasure. Getting your child to read for pleasure is much more than getting them to the point where they can read independently, and your role in this is really, really important. Let the school take the lead on teaching reading and support the school in this by listening to your child read their school books. However, your focus should be primarily on instilling the love of reading. If the focus is on the pleasure of it and children grow to love it, the rest will follow. Together with the school you will create a reader.

> Children who have parental support at home and read for pleasure have a much wider range of vocabulary, and their verbal reasoning is much more advanced than those who do not. Their education journey is going to be much more rapid than those children who don't read for pleasure.
>
> *East Midlands primary school teacher*

📖 Reclaim quiet time

Our children's lives are conspicuously lacking in quiet time and this is, of course, when reading happens. Lack of quiet time is probably one of the biggest challenges to children's reading for pleasure today, so carve out time when all screens are off (including your own!) and when interruptions are kept to a minimum.

📖 Understand today's child

Parents often say to me 'I don't understand why my child doesn't read because I used to love it so much.' I can say with certainty if you contrast your own childhood with your child's you can see why: after-school clubs, homework, 24/7 on-tap entertainment from consoles, phones, laptops and television – all these things compete successfully with reading.

Think about when you were a child. You will have some memories of technology, but how much will depend on how old you are! In the 1970s your family might have played the tennis game Pong through the TV, in the 1980s you may have played Space Invaders in arcades or had an Amstrad computer. Gradually through the 1990s and beyond, more families got PCs and computer gaming gained in popularity.

But whatever you had access to, I can guarantee there is vastly more of it in your child's world now. You would have had plenty of time where there was not much to do, when you were at a loose end and so would have picked up a book. I think many adults who love to read quite possibly came to it in the first place for want of anything else to do. This isn't as odd as it might sound: reading is nothing more than a habit, and like all habits it needs time to establish itself.

> **EXPERT VIEW**
>
> Today, there is a reduction in reading print texts (books, magazines, etc.) and a significant increase in screen time. An argument can be made that children are reading lots on screen – instructions, social media messages – but it is the reading of extended texts that is diminishing, in other words books that take ideas and develop them over a sequence of episodes or sections. Children have to learn that not all reading can be done in bite-size pieces but that there is pleasure, purpose and deeper fulfilment in longer reading experiences.
>
> *David Reedy*

Of course, time is the one thing our children don't have a lot of and screen time is the handiest and quickest fix when boredom strikes. Our children have so little time when their minds can be still, the likelihood of them picking up a book for ten minutes or an hour is so much less than when we were growing up. Reading needs quiet time to take root and grow. Since lives today are very short of this we need to create that time for our children. So, don't book activities after school every day, have a day or two when reading is the thing to look forward to.

📖 Help them with reading choices

Ensuring your child has plenty of reading choices is an important part of helping your child love reading. If there are new and exciting things to read, this should be a great encouragement. The trouble is, although there is a huge variety of books to choose from, many children don't get to see them. Many retailers only stock the big names and high-profile newly published books. There is a vast choice behind all this, available in so many different places.

Have a look in libraries and charity and secondhand shops; talk to teachers, friends, your child's friends and their parents; or go online to look at reading platforms there. The world really is awash with good and interesting things to read – booksellers do not have a monopoly on this. And remember, all reading is good reading, so include comics, magazines, graphic novels, even newspapers as they get older.

As your child develops interests you can pick up on these as ways into reading. Everything they enjoy can be used to inspire them to read, from interests and hobbies to having favourite authors and choosing more by the same person, to getting into a series and working through it, to reading books that mirror experiences like the first time on a plane or at the dentist. Once you start thinking about all the things your child experiences and is involved in, you will find inspiration for new reading material.

Think about what interests your child and what he or she is good at. Whatever it is, you will be sure to find something appealing to read that reflects their enthusiasms. This should motivate them and inspire them to read. Of course interests come and go, but there is always something to reflect their current fascination or obsession. Here are some suggestions of different types of reading material for a range of ages. This list is really the tip of the iceberg; there is masses of choice out there, both fiction and information books, and something interesting for even the most picky child to read. I do hope it gives you some ideas.

• If your child loves to draw, do jigsaw puzzles or read maps, then they might enjoy books with maps, lots of illustrations and interactivity. At picture book age *The Jolly Postman* might fit the bill; at older ages the *Tintin* series or Shaun Tan books such as *The Arrival*. Try the Big Picture Press' *Maps* book.

• If your child loves being active, playing sport, dancing, or doing things with their hands, try books about children that are like them. Perhaps the *Football Academy* series, or a classic such as *Ballet Shoes*. For non-fiction consider *The Football Book* or *Stitch-by-Stitch*.

• If they are obsessed with a character on TV, look out for books and magazines about them.

• If your child loves music and rhythm, read them nursery rhyme books when they are young, and poems as they get older. Try the *Jump up and Join in* books by Carrie and David Grant. Rhyming picture books are fantastic, for example *Cats Ahoy* by Peter Bently, anything by Julia Donaldson, *The Giant Jam Sandwich* by John Vernon Lord and Janet

Burroway. For older children, *Old Possum's Book of Practical Cats* by T. S. Eliot is great fun.

• If they love interacting with people, then books about families and friendship might click: *My Big Shouting Day!* by Rebecca Patterson, *Dave and the Tooth Fairy* by Verna Allette Wilkins, *Hubert Horatio Bartle Bobton-Trent* by Lauren Child, *Dogger* by Shirley Hughes, *The Most Impossible Parents* by Brian Patten, *Grandpa Chatterji* by Jamila Gavin or *Coming to England* by Floella Benjamin. For teens, try books such as *The Greengage Summer* by Rumer Godden or *The L-Shaped Room* by Lynne Reid Banks.

• If your child loves words and enjoys playing with words and sounds, you could try *Silly Verse for Kids* by Spike Milligan, *Noisy Poems* by Jill Bennett, or Roald Dahl's *Revolting Rhymes*.

• If your child loves gaming, there are even books about that too – strategy books for older children, guide books and so on. Try the *Minecraft* books.

• If they are fascinated about how things work, plenty of factual books fit the bill. Try the Usborne *See Inside* series. Or Egmont's *In One End and Out the Other*.

• If your child is logical and analytical, likes to experiment and solve puzzles, then at a young age they might like search and find books. When they get older consider puzzle books: try *Logic Puzzles* by Sarah Khan, and for teens perhaps mysteries such as *The Curious Incident of the Dog in the Night-time* by Mark Haddon, or *Mummies: Mysteries of the Ancient World* by Paul Harrison.

• If your child is fascinated by the natural world then factual nature books might click. For example *Is a Blue Whale the Biggest Thing There Is?* by Robert E. Wells, and for the older child *My Family and Other Animals* by Gerald Durrell. Also try books about animals, such as *Hammy the Wonder Hamster* by Poppy Harris and *Varjak Paw* by S. F. Said.

• If they love a film or TV series, seek out the book it's based on, for example *The Hobbit* by J. R. R. Tolkien, *The Hunger Games* by Suzanne Collins and *Tracy Beaker* by Jacqueline Wilson.

• If your child is technology mad, see if reading digitally is inspiring for them. Got a teen who loves their phone and texting? Try *Txtng: The Gr8 Db8* by David Crystal.

For more suggestions see pages 152–4.

EXPERT VIEW

Finding the right hook to engage a child in a book is difficult to plan as it may depend on the child's mood at the time. However, you can validate their interests and personalities by introducing books that reflect their interests and that are accessible for them in terms of vocabulary and sentence structure. This will pay dividends and help with holistic development, not just literacy. Books with characters that a child can relate to can enhance inter- and intra-personal intelligence and those with problems to solve can develop logical thinking skills. Visually descriptive books, with maps and routes, can engage spatial intelligence skills, and traditional goody and baddy books can promote the development of morality.

Dr Amanda Gummer

Help Your Child Love Reading is a book born out of my passionate belief that establishing a love of reading for pleasure is one of the greatest gifts you can give your child. I know my own experience as a mum and that of others I meet in the course of my work bear this out completely. If there is one thing that comes of writing this book, I'd like it to be for parents to realise their involvement really really matters. You absolutely can make a difference to your child's enjoyment of reading and it will bring your family so much happiness. I wish you every success. Believe me, it's worth it.

Alison David, May 2014

You may have tangible wealth untold,
Caskets of jewels and coffers of gold.
Richer than I, you can never be –
I had a Mother who read to me.

'The Reading Mother', Strickland Gillilan

Chapter 1: Screen time

EXPERT VIEW

Recreational screen time is children's main waking activity. By the age of seven, the average child born today will have spent one full year of 24-hour days watching recreational screen media. It's hardly a coincidence that at the same time reading continues to decline.

Dr Aric Sigman, biologist and psychologist

L urking behind every parent's anxiety about reading and school work is the dreaded screen. It seems to hold a magnetic attraction for children (and adults) and has infiltrated our lives at a furious pace and across all age groups.

Our children spend a lot of time in front of screens. There are various studies and statistics bandied around – for instance, an average of 1 in every 12 waking minutes, or 6.5 hours a day (that's 20 years of your life by the time you reach 80!) are spent in front of a screen. Whatever it is, it's certainly a lot and in some families it is taking over leisure time completely with the result that there is little time left for other things.

There's no doubt that the digital world offers our children exciting entertainment, education and stimulation. Children can learn logic, quick thinking, problem solving and strategy from gaming, and much socialising is now done through texting and social media. But I think screen time should be part of a rich and varied childhood and not dominate our children's lives – certainly if you want your child to do other things, and especially if you want them to read.

Lots of parents tell me they would like their child to spend less time on digital entertainment and more time reading, as well as enjoying other things such as playing outside, getting involved with sport, taking part in imaginary and creative play, enjoying their toys, interacting with other children and so on. In other words, not spending the vast majority of their time in front of a screen.

The truth is that time spent on screen-based entertainment is eroding or even replacing time for other things. Parents I talk to have conflicting emotions about all this. Despite feeling anxious about it they see their children are happy, having fun, socialising with their friends, becoming more and more tech savvy. And that has got to be a good thing in this day and age, hasn't it? So this is really not an easy problem to tackle.

Spending so much time in front of a screen also means children have become accustomed to immediate entertainment. They are growing up with the instant gratification that comes from digital attractions. This is one of the reasons that reading holds less appeal for children today. The ultimate reward from completing a good book is enormous, but it is not instant – it takes a while and some effort to get there. Watching television or YouTube, on the other hand, is a passive activity. Entertainment is presented fully formed and all children have to do is watch it. Gaming and texting are interactive but are also instant – and responses to actions, such as levelling up, winning a game and responses to texts all tend to come thick and fast.

EXPERT VIEW

Gaming produces a burst of the brain's reward chemical dopamine, a substance implicated in all addictions. Interestingly, although 'computer game addiction' is being increasingly recognised by the medical profession, they do not recognise 'book addiction'. And while health departments now recommend limits on children's screen time, curiously they're not recommending a limit on reading time or number of books kept in the child's bookcase. There are a growing number of in-patient clinics for computer addiction, yet there are no Roald Dahl rehab clinics. This is because reading is a very different and more timely neurological and intellectual process, requiring far more inference and cognitive work on the part of the developing child.

Dr Aric Sigman

And gaming and texting only really need short bursts of concentration. Reading requires effort and attention to make sense of the text and follow the story. In other words, it requires sustained concentration.

So not only is it less effort to passively absorb TV programmes, watch videos and to play computer games, but also the rewards come quicker. And the more children do these things, the more their brains become accustomed to them, the more they want and expect that kind of entertainment, and the harder it is for them to concentrate for a longer period of time on something like reading without being distracted.

The moving image of screen entertainment is the perfect medium to produce strong rewards for paying attention to something. Compared to the pace with which real life unfolds and is experienced by young children, screen entertainment portrays life with the fast-forward button fully pressed. Rapidly changing images, scenery and events – zooms, pans and edits – and high-fidelity sounds are highly stimulating and, of course, extremely interesting. Once you are used to food with E numbers and flavour enhancers, real food doesn't taste as interesting. Modern screen entertainment is the flavour enhancer of the audio-visual world, providing unnatural levels of sensory stimulation. Nothing in real life is comparable to this. Screen entertainment overpays the young child to pay attention to it, and in so doing it may corrupt the reward system that enables that child to pay attention to other things in life, such as books.

Dr Aric Sigman

There is no doubt in my mind that the desire for screen time can be compulsive. It can also become obsessive, and I think it's not too strong to say that then it is like a drug. In the worst cases, studies have shown that the changes addiction makes to the brain of an internet addict are similar to those of a drug or alcohol addict: X-rays reveal that pathways to the parts of the brain associated with emotions, decision-making and self-control are interrupted. So these addicts might present as being unable to connect emotionally outside a video game, for instance. At the time of writing it's estimated that 5–10 per cent of internet users are unable to control their usage and are considered addicts. These numbers are small and the point I make is extreme, but the power of screen-based entertainment to hook us is abundantly clear in our daily lives. And other studies have found a significant link between excessive social networking usage and depression.

As a parent, I know you'll have seen the big negative impact – physically, mentally and emotionally – that *excessive* screen time can have on your child. All the families I have talked to, without exception, have observed changes in their children's behaviour after too much screen time, whether it be TV, gaming or texting. These changes range from being mildly obsessive, over-excited or lacking in concentration on other things, through to being moody, bad-tempered, hyperactive or even outright aggressive when told it's time to switch off the machine.

Children can get fixated when trying to get past the next level in a game, checking social media updates, replying to texts or watching the next instalment of something on YouTube. Like addicts they can lose interest in other things as a result. Think about your own need to keep checking emails or your phone for texts. How hard do you find it to switch off and be still, to concentrate on reading? I know how hard it is for me. It's the same, if not worse, for children.

EXPERT VIEW

Children are understandably influenced by sensation-seeking and instant gratification without their impulse control being fully developed, and so their ability to self-regulate their own screen time is extremely limited.

Dr Aric Sigman

How screens are used for entertainment in the home is therefore a vital element in your child's reading development. If you want your child to read for pleasure, you'll need to give the whole issue a lot of thought, not only considering the negative aspects of digital entertainment, the internet and computers, but also the positive ones.

> He plays on his Xbox before breakfast, after breakfast and after school. We'd like him to focus his energies into other things but it's like fighting a losing battle.
>
> *Parents to Jordan, age 12*

Reading for pleasure and recreational screen time can co-exist. I have met families where reading thrives despite all the distractions on offer, and you'll be pleased to know it's not that difficult to achieve, although it does require some determination. If you want your child to read for pleasure you have to limit screen time, both to make space and time for reading and to help your child to focus and concentrate on enjoying a good story.

If there are no rules in place to control the amount of screen time, reading for pleasure will definitely suffer because children won't have the interest, time, patience or attention span to read a book.

I sometimes think the principles of helping your child read for pleasure are like raising a healthy eater – we realise if we want a healthy-eating child we have to supply the good stuff, encourage them to try new things, offer a range of foods and restrict the bad stuff. We don't let them eat chocolate until they are sick, or drink Coke until they are ill, but we do let them have sweets from time to time. Raising a reader and managing screen time is the same.

📖 Finding a balance

The really important point is that it's not about denying children screen time but it is about being clear on what is allowed. It's about finding a balance. Your child needs to know screen time is a treat or a privilege, but not their right to use as they wish. Children don't know what is best for them, and left without rules they won't turn off the TV, Xbox or Wii because, as I said before, they do not self-regulate. Screen time will take over if children are free to choose.

> I think my nephew thinks all mobile phones are his by rights! As soon as I go through the front door he says 'Can I have your phone?' before he even says hello to me. Apparently he says this to all the adults he meets. I know his mum has regular dramas of having to physically wrestle with him to get her phone back. He's only 3!
>
> *Angela, aunt to Lukas*

It's certainly made harder to find balance by the sheer number of devices a child typically has access to. I talked to a dad who likened restricting screen time for his children to holding back a tsunami. He told me that at home they have Sky TV, a PC, a laptop, mobiles, a Nintendo DS, a Wii and an Xbox, and the children are constantly badgering for time on screen, be it playing games or using social media to talk to friends. And technology is developing so fast. If you have a young baby now as well as an older child, you will be aware of the huge difference in the digital entertainment available to your baby. One mum I talked to told me she could see a massive increase between her 15 month old's gadgets and pre-school apps and what her 8 year old had access to at that age.

📖 Having rules

So, how do you strike that balance? The most obvious and best place to start is by establishing some basic rules. Marking out boundaries is a positive thing for children – they know what is expected of them and it makes them feel secure. They also know that when they have kept to the rules they have done well. But so many families I meet feel they can't, or don't want to, say no to their children about screen time. I think they confuse having rules about it with punishment. When you restrict screen time you are not punishing your child, you are creating space and time to do other things. Rules about screen time teach self-control and discipline.

> Our children all read a lot. My wife has a real gift for finding interesting books and we are very strict with computers and mobile phones. If they had no restrictions they would probably stop reading immediately!
>
> *Dad to Claire, age 15, Eva, age 13 and Luke, age 7*

You need also to establish consequences if the rules are broken: if you have set a limit of one hour for gaming and your child won't stop at the end of it, you can cut the amount of time when he next uses the machine or even take away the privilege.

You are in charge. That is the only time when taking away screen time is a punishment; the rules themselves aren't.

📖 Ideas and suggestions for rules

I can't tell you exactly what rules to establish because they have to be workable for you and your family. But I can share effective ideas that I have come across in my conversations with numerous families.

Reading will most definitely suffer if there are screens in the bedroom. Research among 4,000 pupils in England found children with TVs in their bedrooms and children who own their own mobile phones suffered significant falls in reading achievement. So, do not have screens in the bedroom: no TV, no computer, no DVD player and no consoles. As your children get older and get mobile phones, make sure they are removed from their rooms at bedtime. If your child needs a computer for homework and works in their own room, consider getting a laptop, so that it can be put somewhere else at bedtime.

EXPERT VIEW

Increasing screen time is about access and consumption. Think about it, if you put a fridge in your child's bedroom they're likely to eat more. And if you told them one compartment had broccoli and sprouts, and the other had Ben & Jerry's, your child is likely to eat more and it won't be those healthy vegetables on offer.

Dr Aric Sigman

Limit school-day screen time. I met a family who have a rule that says no recreational screen time at all from

Monday to Thursday – although of course if the children need to do homework on the computer that is allowed. Their children accept this. I have also met a family who allow their 12 year old 45 minutes in the evening, but only after their homework is done.

At weekends you might want to give a longer time for screens – maybe even up to 2–3 hours at a stretch as a maximum for teenagers. At younger ages you should probably reduce this amount of time but, again, adapt this to your child. Watch how they behave and feel after an extended period of play and change the time if necessary.

Turn off screens (including TV) at least 30 minutes before bedtime to give your child a chance to wind down and to give them a decent amount of time to read.

When you are dealing with very young children who don't understand the concept of time, using an alarm or timer of some sort can be very useful. You could say they are allowed 30 minutes and when the alarm goes off, time is up. I used this strategy very successfully with my son when he was younger and he would simply turn off the laptop when the bell rang, no questions asked.

For older children who better understand time, it's very useful to give a 5– or 10–minute warning that time is nearly up.

Make sure that your child asks if they can use the computer or games console before they turn it on. This reinforces that it is a privilege and not a right. You can answer 'yes', or 'no', 'later', 'yes, for 30 minutes', or 'yes, if you've done your homework' – whatever matches the rules you've laid down or agreed.

Even if you have no problems restricting screen time with your child at the moment and an informal, ad hoc arrangement seems to work just fine, or if they are young and perhaps not especially keen on digital entertainment as yet, I urge you to think ahead. Imagine your child is young, say four, and from time to time she wants to play on your iPhone. You let her do that and when you say that's enough she complies. There is no problem. Before long she won't comply, however, as she finds her voice and more firmly forms her likes and dislikes. Children grow up. So just make sure when you say 'Yes, you can play on the iPhone', you give a time limit too. For instance: 'You can play on the iPhone for ten minutes, then we'll get the crayons out, or we'll read a book.'

If you establish house rules about screen time now, you will be well set as and when demands for more screen time come your way, which inevitably they will. Do this and your child will grow up accepting there is no unfettered access to screens.

📖 Establishing rules for older children

If your child is older – say age eight upwards – and you are intending to introduce screen time rules, be prepared for the fact that your child may not take it well. How cross they get will in part depend on their age and how long they have been accustomed to doing what you want to restrict. I can only say stick to your guns! Older children may be more difficult to manage but that's normal because they are learning about life, that things don't always go their way, and they do have to learn that when you say no, you mean it.

If your child complains that everyone else in their class can play all evening or that their best friend can spend as much time as they like, your reply must be something along the lines of 'Every family has rules and these are our rules.' I remember being with a family who had no set rules about screen time and it backfired on them. Their daughter was happily playing on her DS and her mum said, apparently out of the blue, 'Turn it off, you've had enough now.' Of course, the girl made a huge fuss and there was a family row because she saw it as her mum ruining her fun. Because there was no warning before the time was up, the girl didn't feel in control. An easier way for all involved would have been to tell her up front that she had a certain amount of time and give her a five–minute warning before the time was up.

Remember that children ultimately like boundaries; they like to know they have been good, and you make it easy for them to be good and be praised by having rules to stick to. To be honest, you will find it a whole lot easier if you set up screen time rules from a young age when children are less rebellious and more accepting. You can then adapt them as your child grows and you will be in a much better position to keep them enforced when they reach their teens and seem to want to immerse themselves in digital entertainment and not much else. If your children are more mature and you think you can reason with them effectively, why not sit down and agree the time limits with them?

📖 Digital reading

When I talk about reading throughout this book I am usually not making a distinction between physical books and digital books. After all, the content is the same, it's just the delivery method that is different. The same sustained concentration is required to read an extended piece of writing, whether on paper or screen.

Although adult e-reading is gaining ground, up to now children's e-reading has been slower to get going. It will no doubt speed up as more devices become available. However, you might find your child is keen to read on a digital device. If so, that's great, especially if they are older. I would caution against using digital books at a young age. Let your child enjoy the feel of physical books, the pleasure of being able to hold them, flick through them and carry them around. This is all part and parcel of the reading experience.

Also, keeping the physical book as a reminder of shared reading as your child gets older is a contributory factor to the relationship glue I talk about elsewhere in the book. I remember so clearly some of the books my mum and I read together when I was growing up, some of which were kept and I was able to read to my son. I'm especially fond of a dog-eared copy of *The House at Pooh Corner*. And my brother gave my son, on loan, his treasured childhood copy of *Wilf Weasel's Speedy Skates*, which was treated with great reverence by Louis. That physical continuity is not something you get with e-books. So I think it would be a shame to miss out on the physical presence of books in the early years, quite apart from any developmental harm screen time might cause.

Screen time is a very modern problem. Finding the balance between recognising the utility of computers and the potential developmental impairment that overuse can cause is one of the most common issues in family life nowadays. Health education specialists like Dr Aric Sigman, as well as the Department of Health, are raising awareness among parents of the need to consider discretionary and recreational screen time as yet another form of consumption – similar to sweets or crisps, or hours in direct sunshine – that is measured in minutes or hours per day, and which needs to be thought about and limited. There is no way around it; you do need to get involved to help your child find that balance.

Here's an example of how you go about finding the balance. One mum told me her son, Alfie, is an avid gamer. He is seven years old and into playing the same games on the Wii and on the iPad as much as his friends are. But he is also a very keen reader. She said 'Alfie reads to relax. He reads in bed every day – we have a routine. He is not allowed to have any gaming kit or phone or TV in his room.'

It can be done!

Chapter 2: Pre-school

*Children are made readers
on the laps of their parents.*

Emilie Buchwald, author and publisher

I remember so clearly the moment I arrived home with my newborn son. The love I felt for him was so overwhelming that I felt I'd loved him all my life, as if there was a bit of me missing until he came along. I remember all I wanted to do was hold him hour after hour, day after day, awake or asleep, it didn't matter. I was also anxious – about keeping him safe, about doing things the right way, about making him happy. There was so much to cherish and yet so much to worry about that all those idealised pictures in my mind of a child who never cried and who slept through the night were quickly banished. Getting through each day and night was enough of a challenge.

I took comfort though that at least one thing was under my control. I would read to him regardless of the stresses and strains of the day. From the earliest possible age, my mum read to me and to my two brothers. I remember listening to her read *Mrs Nibble Moves House* so many times, and even now, in her seventies, she can still recite it perfectly. She instilled the love of reading in my brothers and myself. So it never occurred to me not to read to Louis. I wanted him to love books, like I did, from the very beginning and experience the same pleasure that they gave me. I wanted to share my love of reading with him. It was just like feeding him, like feeding his mind.

The Reading Habit

The pre-school years are a time of extraordinary change that is profound and satisfying both for parents and children. In the beginning, babies seem to require you only to be a feeding, bathing and nappy-changing machine. Later, as toddlers, they demand constant interaction and attention for a game they have just invented, over and over and over again. The rate with which they learn new skills and exhibit more and more personality is excitingly exhausting.

For your child, every day is full of strange, new things. Magic and fantasy are real – the monster really is under the bed, the tooth fairy does bring shiny coins and Father Christmas somehow knows exactly what every child wants. This is a time when new and unexpected things happen frequently, the world constantly changes and hundreds of new experiences come along every week.

These new experiences can be exciting but they can also be bewildering and frightening. It's no wonder then that young children cling to routine to help them feel safe, secure and confident to face the new adventures. And you need to create the routines for them.

One of the questions I'm asked most often by parents is when they should start reading to their child. The short answer is 'as soon as you possibly can'. Setting up a reading routine can be a bit of a struggle in these early weeks and months but, once firmly embedded in family life, will bring joy, calm and a shared interest that will last for years. With my son, after we'd got over the initial first few weeks, we built reading into the rhythm of our family life as soon as we could. Years later and we have maintained that rhythm, and the reading bond that we created together when he was born is as strong as ever.

<table>
<tr><td>EXPERT VIEW</td><td>The single most important thing that a parent can do to help their child acquire language, prepare their child for school, and instil a love of learning in their child, is to read to them.

Do parents know they matter?, Russ et al., 2007</td></tr>
</table>

To get the reading habit, the most important thing is to make reading a central part of your daily routine. Use every opportunity you can find to read to your child – when they are feeding, when they are in the bath and when they are being cuddled. I know of one family that propped a book by their baby's head when the nappy was being changed. Even if you only have a chance to read once a day, make sure that you do. At this stage it doesn't actually matter what you read. Hearing voices reading to them, singing nursery rhymes together and associating looking at books with the comfort and security of being with parents are what is important.

I was so excited when our daughter was born and I wanted to do so much from the very moment she came home. But in those very early days, I can remember feeling quite excluded from the relationship between my daughter and partner. While I helped out as much as I could, supporting my partner when she was feeding and when she needed to sleep, I just didn't feel the same strength of bond that she and my daughter had. By starting to read to her at bedtime, in the bath, when we were relaxing in the living room or when we were out, I managed to establish my part in the daily routine — and the reading habit has lasted well into her early teenage years.

Martin, dad to Hannah

Having established a rhythm and routine, you have laid the foundations for your reading life together. And here are some easy ways to make them stronger.

📖 Remember that books are very portable!

Pack a book or two in the changing bag, or sling one into the tray of the buggy when you go out. There's always a moment when you can sit down and grab a few minutes' reading time.

📖 Reinforce what you read

Link things that you see with books you have read when you are out and about. If you see a cat, or a fire engine, a bus or someone walking a dog, point it out to your child and remind them of that story. Suggest reading the book again when you get home. Just as you instinctively look out for objects that could harm your child, develop the reflex to spot and mention resemblances to stories you have read together. If you have read *The Tiger Who Came to Tea*, say, 'I wonder if that's the tiger coming to tea' when the doorbell rings and then read the book with them again later. Or if you see a worm in the garden, remind your child of the *Mr Jelly* story where he thinks a worm is a snake. Then read the book again and say 'Remember, we saw a worm today just like the one in the book.'

Books that invite playful interaction between parent and child really do work in developing reading as a pleasurable experience. For instance, try reading a book that shows exactly what 'tickle' means first-hand. The interaction, pictures and repetitive text can make it so much fun.

In these and other ways you make stories an integral part of your child's life. These are just a few examples, but it's very easy to do. Look for books that your child can relate to and soon you'll find that you naturally pick up on things you see together and the references will become part of your family language and a shared memory to enjoy.

📖 Instil positive associations

Whenever you sit down to read, introduce the idea with positive language – for example, 'Let's read a lovely book' – so that the association of reading with pleasure, comfort and security is firmly established.

EXPERT VIEW

Positive reinforcement is the most powerful tool a parent has, and making reading a positive experience will pay dividends.

Dr Amanda Gummer, child development expert

As your children get older and start to make choices about what they'd like to read with you, avoid negative comments like 'Oh no, not that one again!' Always keep any comments you make positive. This is all about infecting them with the reading bug and encouraging the pleasure of reading and story. This can sometimes mean that you have to think positively when having to read something you do not enjoy much. I remember my heart sinking when the choice was a reference book about the Thunderbirds machines. My 'job' was to read all the annotations on the diagrams of the engines, interiors and equipment!

> **EXPERT VIEW**
>
> You might draw attention to the printed word as your child gets older, and reaches two, three and four years old. You could say things like, 'Look, those words say "Elmer the elephant". Let's see if we can spot the word Elmer again.' You should wait until you have read the book a few times to your child before you try this. Or when you're out and about make the connection between print and what you see and your child's experience. For example, 'Look Sophie, Sainsbury's starts with an S just like your name!'
>
> *David Reedy, literacy expert*

If you are working and therefore away from your child all day, use books and reading as a treat. Say 'I'll be back later and we can play, and read some books, won't that be great?' In this way reading becomes associated with happy times and something for you both to look forward to.

📖 Say 'no' to screens

Getting the reading habit will sometimes require saying 'no' to the television or iPad – both to yourself (it's so easy just to let them have ten minutes while you make that phone call or send that email) and to your child. The problem is that a phone or iPad is so accessible to a child that it is hard to always keep them out of reach.

Children need to be shown that first and foremost books are about enjoyment; that learning is a happy, almost effortless by-product.
Michael Morpurgo, author

In the past year alone, smartphone and tablet use by children has grown hugely; this at a time when the number of pre-school children reading for pleasure (choosing to pick up a book) each week has dropped from 64 per cent to 57 per cent in one year.

A study in 2013 showed that tablet usage is now at 18 per cent for 0–2 year olds (up from 7 per cent in 2012); at 28 per cent for 3–4 year olds (up from 16 per cent) and there has been a similar climb in smartphone usage. Now 20 per cent of 0–2 year olds use them, while the figure is closer to a third for 3–4 year olds, up from 15 per cent and 25 per cent respectively in the previous year.

'The UK Children's Book Consumer in the Digital Age', *Bowker 2013*

EXPERT VIEW

While it's important to embrace technology and help children prepare for life in an increasingly technological world, it's important to use tech toys to enhance engagement with reading and learning, and not replace it. It's helpful to think of screen time in the same way as sweets and treats when planning a diet. Balance is key and treats should be limited and counterbalanced with lots of healthy activites and nutrition.

Dr Amanda Gummer

The long-term benefits of the reading habit though will far, far outweigh the short-term peace you gain if you allow screen time. Books and reading, instead of screens and watching television, reinforce the idea of shared family identity as well. It shows your child that 'this is how we are in our family'. Reading becomes the norm rather than a chore or the 'less good' option. You can make this stronger, of course, by setting an example and making time to sit down and read yourself. For more information about screens see pages 18–31.

Children who spent more than two hours a day in front of screens were 67 per cent more likely to have more attention problems than their peers.

www.healthcare-today.co.uk

📖 Build on successes and shared stories

Even from an early age, you will see benefits from developing a reading habit.

The more I read to Louis, the more stories seemed to bind us together. I also saw, as he grew, what a profound impact reading was having on his development. His ability to associate things that we saw when we were out and about with the words he'd heard in the stories I read to him became an increasingly joyful part of every outing. I vividly remember one day sitting in a friend's kitchen with Louis, who was about 16 months old at the time. The wallpaper had a butterfly theme and he pointed to it and said 'apergee', his version of 'caterpillar'. I looked at the wallpaper and was amazed that he'd made the connection between butterfly and caterpillar. Then I remembered that we had just been reading *The Very Hungry Caterpillar* in which the caterpillar transforms into a beautiful butterfly. When I realised that he had been able to use the information from our reading together in a real-life situation, it made me read to him even more!

📖 Use character stories

> Reading aloud to young children is not only one of the best activities to stimulate language and cognitive skills; it also builds motivation, curiosity, and memory.
>
> from *Talk to Me, Baby!* by Betty Bardige

A good way of helping children to settle down to read or be read to is to use books based on their favourite television or film characters. One parent told me that her son, aged three, is obsessed with watching *Peppa Pig* on TV but is very resistant to having a book read to him. 'Reading *Peppa Pig* books at bedtime – his firm and constant favourite! – and one or two others of our choosing has provided us with a good bedtime routine,' she says. 'He will now settle down and enjoy the books.'

Connecting with characters

EXPERT VIEW

Children connect with characters either because they identify with them and they can see themselves in the characters' storylines, or because they provide an escape from a child's known world and allow them the freedom of imagination.

Dr Amanda Gummer

There are four ways that children connect with characters: they do it through reflection, emulation, nurturing and dis-identification. Characters may reflect children's own lives and aspirations, help them learn and be a comfort – all reasons why stories about favourite characters can make a really deep impression.

Reflection   A child recognises a character's traits in themselves, or relates a story and situation with their own life. When they see the character as 'like me' they naturally identify with the character and story. *Thomas the Tank Engine* is a good example – he means well but gets it wrong sometimes. Piglet, from *Winnie-the-Pooh*, is the reflection of a young child because he is small in size but capable of great things! Piglet gets scared and makes mistakes, but he also shows great bravery and real loyalty to his friends.

Emulation   This means the child wants to be like the character in some way. These characters portray some real emotions that the child can identify with, but their lifestyle or existence puts them higher on a pedestal than a reflective character. *Ben 10* and *Mr Strong* are good examples. If a child can emulate a character, then this is a very powerful connection. Superheroes of course are classic examples. As an aside, I think it's pretty obvious why gaming appeals so much when you consider this. A child can take on, via the game, the persona of a character that they admire.

Nurturing   Children up to the age of about 12 still seek a certain safety in characters and stories. Connecting through nurturing can either be allowing a child to look after a character and be the 'grown up', or it can come through in the ability a character has to look after the audience. One example is Kanga, again from *Winnie-the-Pooh*, who not only nurtures Roo but gives the stories a warm security and sense of reassurance.

Dis-identification   This allows the child to explore their darker side, either through baddies or through a good character's naughty behaviour. The latter allows a child to draw parallels with real life. They see the consequences of a character's actions and apply what they learn to their own lives. *Horrid Henry*, *Little Miss Naughty* and Naughty Norman from *Fireman Sam* are all good examples.

Boys

Boys can find it hard to sit still and listen to stories because they tend to be much more active. At four years old, a boy's testosterone level surges and doubles. At this age they become interested in action, heroics and vigorous play. You can capitalise on this by choosing books about action heroes, books where actions are needed, where you can shout out and increase the energy levels.

> I just had a report from Oscar's nursery telling me he spends more than normal amounts of time looking at books. It's so great to hear. I have read to him from the minute I brought him home, starting with black-and-white books. He is 15 months now and into everything, so active and busy. The only time he allows me to have him on my knee is when I read to him! He will be still for 20 minutes to half an hour, so I get great cuddles.
>
> *Lou, mum to Oscar*

How to read

It may seem a bit silly to include a section on how to read to your infant or toddler, but there are some tips and techniques that I've learned both from my own experience and from watching and talking to other parents which have really helped maintain a child's interest.

• **Use colour, rhythm and intonation** in your voice to vary the tone. It can be fun to really exaggerate – e.g. a sharp intake of breath to show extreme surprise, or anticipation, or 'OH NO' for any dangerous situation and so on. Ham it up, they'll love it!

• **Use different voices and accents** for different characters. You don't have to be able to pull off a perfect accent. It's enough to vary your voice. Simply make one character speak in a deep voice and the other in a squeaky high voice, for instance.

• **Encourage your child** to complete familiar phrases by pausing before the end of the sentence. They like repetition and love to show they know what is coming next.

• **Spend plenty of time** on the pictures if your child seems to enjoy this. Before they learn to talk you can ask 'What can we see?', and answer 'We can see a bus and a dog …' and so on. As they become more aware, you can ask them 'Where is the frog?', 'Can you see the tractor?', and let them point. As they learn to talk you can ask 'What can you see?' You can also pretend that you can't see something; children love knowing more than you do! Try saying, 'I can't see the frog anywhere, can you?' and then follow them finding the frog with lots of praise.

• **Bring books to life!** If you're going to the seaside, find a relevant book – *Lucy & Tom at the Seaside*, for example. There are many books that tell stories of what happens there. In the *Mr Bump* book he falls into a hole on the beach. You could dig a hole and say that it's for *Mr Bump*, then read the book again either on the beach or at home that evening.

• **Slow down.** We all tend to read too fast when we read aloud. Allow yourself plenty of time to get the most fun out of each word and sentence. It doesn't matter at all if you stumble over some of the words. Remember, your child is really enjoying basking in your undivided attention.

• **You don't have to finish it!** If their attention starts to wander, ask them if they would like a different book – and let them choose.

• **Allow them to munch** on a healthy snack while you're reading.

Parents often ask how much time they should spend reading. Like a lot of things there isn't a straightforward answer to this and much will depend on your child, on when you're reading to them and how much time you have. For very young children, five to ten minutes is perhaps all their attention span can cope with. As they get older and bedtime becomes much more regular, then my advice would be as much time as you can spare. At the age of four, Louis and I were reading four books a night. They were picture books so it was still a manageable amount of time. As we moved on to chapter books we changed the number of books to the number of chapters – to one, two or three depending on the book.

Children who are read to at least three times a week by a family member are almost twice as likely to score in the top 25 per cent in reading as children who are read to less frequently.

'Early Childhood Longitudinal Study', US Department of Education

I also get asked when is the best time to read, to which the simple answer is whenever you can. However, to be practical, fix on one time that you know for certain you can manage every day – bedtime is the most common. The three Bs (Bath, Book, Bed) routine can kick in from an early age and should give you lots of good quality parent–child time.

You can vary who reads – mum, dad, grandparents. Just make it a trusted and loved voice if you can. If there are other points in the day when there is the opportunity to grab your baby, a chair and a book, then take it. Whatever else, make sure there is one time every day when your baby, then toddler, then young child knows they will have a cuddle and a story.

If you're finding it difficult to engage your child with books, take cues from whatever they respond to positively. If they seem to like stories where you can make loud noises, or perform actions, sing or put on funny voices, find more of those kinds of books. You'll find it an interesting way of discovering more about your child's likes and dislikes. As they get older allow them to choose a book to read together; sometimes this means reading the same book over and over and over … and over again! Don't worry about that – they love repetition and it increases their feeling of security.

But if reading the same book every night really does just get too wearing, suggest that they choose one and you choose one. That way they get two books and you get to read something different. (It's also an early introduction to the idea of sharing and co-operation.) Louis says he can remember me reading to him as a toddler and what he liked was that he had 'free choice and was not hindered'. Remember, it's really not that easy being a pre-schooler. Choice is very limited; you have to go to sleep when you're told (sometimes when you're not tired), eat your greens and other disgusting food, share things with other children when you don't want to, and go along with all the things mum and dad say. A bit of independence is cherished by all kids and if you can associate that choice with reading, so much the better.

If your child can't or does not want to choose, that's equally okay. Sometimes too much choice is hard for a pre-schooler. You can try to make it easier for them by offering two books and asking which one they want. I used to find this worked well at the magazine rack in the supermarket too. The choice was too much for Louis sometimes so it was far better to pick out a couple and ask 'Which one do you want, this one or that one?'

The Reading Home

The Reading Home is any home that is full of books, words and stories – written or spoken. Every room has some reading material in it: bathroom, bedroom, kitchen, loo, garden shed. It doesn't matter where you are, books, magazines and other forms of writing are within reach. Books are part of the atmosphere and feel of the home.

There's a simple idea behind this: finding something to read is as easy as, if not easier than, picking up an iPad or turning on the television. If you can't stretch financially to filling the house with books and magazines (or even if you can), then talk about stories, bring them to life, and tell your child stories of the day and try to link characters and places to ones they may have already met in a book. Or borrow from friends: set up a circulating library with friends and other families you met during your pregnancy perhaps. Try charity shops, school fetes, or car boot sales for other sources of cheap books and places to hunt out different kinds of reading material.

And once you have a variety of books at home, make sure you display them with the covers, not the spines, facing out. After all, the covers are designed by publishers to make the biggest impact on children, so don't waste them! There are even bookshelves that you can buy that have been designed to display books face out. When your child is playing in the living room or play room, bring out three or four books – different ones each day – and put them in among the toys. Your child will get used to seeing them around and pick them up independently. Books will become associated with play and, you never know, you might be asked to read one of them outside normal reading time!

As well as having lots of children's books around, even when your child is this young it's important she sees you read for pleasure too. You are her biggest role model and if she sees you reading she will want to emulate you.

Get into the habit of giving books as birthday and Christmas presents. Make it a family tradition that you all get a book and make a point of saying, 'We always get a book at Christmas, don't we?' and then build anticipation, 'I wonder what book you will get in your stocking this year?'

Give books as rewards and treats, and give them to your child's friends for birthday presents. Give your children magazines, too. Show how special and valued reading of any kind is, and that all reading is good reading.

Research based on over 70,000 case studies in 27 countries showed that 'Children growing up in homes with many books get three years more schooling than children from bookless homes, independent of their parents' education, occupation, and class.'

'Books and schooling in 27 nations', Mariah Evans, University of Nevada-Reno, USA

What to read?

For children up to about six months, it really doesn't matter what you read as long as the habit begins. Sing nursery rhymes or even read aloud from the novel or magazine you're currently trying to snatch ten minutes with. The important thing at this stage is the voice and the routine.

After six months, baby and bath books are a better option because repetition and the structure of the book will help engage and entertain them. These books are also designed to withstand a good chewing! As your children get older you'll work out what they like and dislike the more you read together.

If one cannot enjoy reading a book over and over again, there is no use in reading it at all.

Oscar Wilde

You can also use books to help get through new experiences. Going to the dentist, starting playgroup, the arrival of a new brother or sister, or even when you're training them to use the potty – books are great for getting them to stay seated! Publishers have been very good at providing blanket coverage of these occasions: *Topsy and Tim*, the *Maisy* books or the Usborne *First Experiences* series all help young children understand and get through what can sometimes be quite difficult times.

Try lift-the-flap books when your child gets to about one or so. Books such as *Where's Spot?* by Eric Hill and *Dear Zoo* by Rod Campbell are great for developing engagement, anticipation and prediction.

There are loads of funny books available. Children love to laugh, and will ask for their favourites over and over. Again, the jokes in these books can become part and parcel of your shared family language.

If your child shows an interest in the mechanics of reading then help them work out the letter sounds, but there is no pressure for you to teach them to read. Leave that to school when they go there. The reading time at home is all about showing and sharing the pleasure and joy of reading.

Dos and Don'ts

Below are some strategies to adopt to encourage the reading habit in your pre-school child.

Dos

✓ Always read a bedtime story or stories. No exceptions. (Remember the 3 Bs!)

✓ Let them choose the books they want you to read at bedtime.

✓ Read anytime anywhere, but it is also good to have some fixed times too. When your child starts nursery or goes to a child-minder there is a bit more structure to his day so try to establish a regular time to sit down and share a book together.

✓ Sing and read nursery rhymes and poems. Children love rhyme and rhythm.

✓ Always carry books with you when you go out.

✓ Introduce character books at an early stage. Children can identify with their favourite characters and love their own popular culture. Go with it even if you find the purple dinosaur a complete turn-off!

✓ Say no to screen time for as long as you possibly can!

✓ Sometimes ask older siblings, cousins or the neighbours' children to read a story to a younger child. Hearing a child's voice changes the tone and the child's perspective on the story.

✓ When you're out and about, be on the lookout for links back to stories you have read together.

Don'ts

✖ Never, ever use withholding a story as a punishment. Never link it to the negative. You are trying to make reading, stories and books synonymous with pleasure and fun.

✖ Don't ever show boredom with their choice of books.

✖ Do not allow a television or screen in the bedroom. This is a surefire way of sending reading to the bottom of the list of entertainment activities!

A recent US study of 2,623 children found that those who watched TV at the ages of one to three years 'had a significantly increased risk of developing attentional problems by the time they were seven years old.'

Review published in the journal Pediatrics

Q & A

I just don't have the time to sit down and read. There's just too much to do. What can I do?

The length of time isn't as important as the routine. Ten minutes with your child and a book or a magazine every day will pay you and your child back tenfold in the future.

My boy simply won't sit still for more than two minutes. How can I possibly get him to sit on my lap for ten?

Identify the point in the day when he is least active and sit him down then. Give him something to chew on, or to snack or to hold – perhaps a favourite toy. Try bedtime for the particularly wriggly ones.

What if my child can't concentrate for a whole story?

Try books you can dip in and out of – for example, fact books – so that there is no pressure to remember what has already happened in the story. One parent of a very distracted pre-school boy told me that sitting down at bedtime with an atlas cured him of his excessive jumping on the bed and lack of interest in books!

My children are at different stages – how do I read to both of them?

The best way is to allow them to choose one story each for you to read with them individually and one that you can all read together. If you allow them both a choice and alternate which child chooses the book you read together you should keep them both happy. Encourage the older one to help by reading some words or sentences depending on what stage they are at.

Developmental stages

Here are some key milestones in a baby's development during the pre-school years:

FROM BIRTH: reaches for things; laughs; smiles; holds objects in closed fist; develops from seeing in black and white to seeing in colour.

FROM 6 MONTHS: begins to understand sequence (for example, that night follows day); loves repetition; can grab and pull things towards them.

FROM 12 MONTHS: chooses the same book time and time again; starts to use lift-the-flap books; begins to make recognisable word sounds and to respond to name.

FROM 18 MONTHS: begins to use logical reasoning, to sort shapes, to complete puzzles (eight or fewer pieces); develops a sense of rhythm; is attracted by bright colours and by tactile experiences; recognises signs and symbols; can scribble; enjoys repetitive texts with interesting language, sounds and rhyme; follows words on a page and knows sequence; can form three-word sentences that include a verb; can hold a pencil and use a touch screen.

FROM 3 YEARS: Two of five children can name 5–10 letters; enjoys listening to and begins to re-tell simple stories, enjoys rhymes and repetitive stories with recognised characters; can name common objects in picture books or magazines; understands sequence of words (left to right); recognises words in context and that letters on the page represent the sounds of spoken words; has better motor skills – can feed self and starts to understand that others see things in different ways.

NOTE TO PARENTS: the speed of child development varies hugely from child to child and different skills are mastered at different ages – often determined by a child's environment. However, whatever age they acquire these skills, they are acquired in sequence, so children build up more complex skills on the foundations of previously mastered simpler skills. For example, a child cannot learn to write using fine motor skills until he or she has mastered the gross motor skills that underpin the muscle development. Above all, remember no two children are the same!

Chapter 3: Starting School

Books shouldn't be daunting, they should be funny, exciting and wonderful; and learning to be a reader gives a terrific advantage.

Roald Dahl

Something happens in many families as soon as the children start school – parents step back from reading stories with them. I have seen it countless times. A bewildering mass of new things to think about and to experience overwhelms the well-established routines of the pre-school years. In among the packed lunches, school runs, play dates and after-school exhaustion, the shared pleasure of sitting down with a book gets lost. Reading to your child for fun is overtaken by the understandable drive to make children independent readers. Reading becomes less about story and more about skill. Worryingly, this is also the point at which we start to see the steep drop off in children being read to.

The start of school also lets new outside factors into your home life – other children and their parents, different ways of doing things, different ways of playing. All of these are fantastic as long as the reading habit you have nurtured (or want to create) is not lost along the way.

EXPERT VIEW

It is so important that the reading routine established before children start school continues long after. We know for sure that children who are read to after the age of five read for pleasure more often themselves and do better at school in lots of subjects, not just English, all the way through primary and secondary school.

David Reedy, literacy expert

This chapter is all about how you manage your child's transition from home, child-minder or nursery to school. It is important that you know how to maintain a balance for your child between learning the mechanics of reading independently and keeping alive the joy of reading for its own sake.

Your child at school

This is such an exhilarating moment: your child is going to start school and in the first few years learn how to read. Most children find learning to read exciting, and parents are thrilled by their progress. Lots of children pass through the transition painlessly, learning bit by bit and enjoying the journey. For others it's not much fun at all. They may find it hard and confidence-sapping. For a few, the process can even turn them off reading altogether.

Many parents also find this time hard-going. Routines need to change, your child is often exhausted and fractious by the end of the school day, and there is less time in the evenings to do all the things you want and need to do. There is the additional worry and frustration of wanting your child to become an independent reader both for their own pleasure and, let's be honest, for your own sake as well. Reading to them will be one less thing to do in the small amount of time available every evening. Balancing the demands of their lives with work and everything else in your own busy life becomes more and more difficult. So finding the time and energy to maintain or create the reading habit is often not an appealing prospect!

Added to this, school reading is a very different exercise from the cosy pre-school picture-book-reading years. Think about it from your child's point of view: until they start school, the time you spend reading to them is time when they can relax, enjoy your undivided attention, and take in the fun and magic of the story. Once they start school, it can seem like there has been a U-turn on reading. They may get a message, very early on, that reading is now a task to be learned – and often a pressurised one at that.

Many children come home from school with the statement that they have to read for 15 to 20 minutes every night. There is no choice involved. Although your child's teacher is saying this because reading aloud is one of the most effective strategies in learning to read and understanding what's been read, the 'have to' part can turn some children off.

There are two ways to tackle this: first, it might sound obvious but make sure your child likes the school book. If they don't, explain this to the teacher and try substituting something more appealing, perhaps silly or funny, to motivate them. Second, don't use bedtime stories for school reading. I have met a lot of parents who unwittingly take away their child's pleasure by killing two birds with one stone and making the compulsory school reading into the bedtime story – focusing on them getting the reading task done rather than the pleasure of the story. Before they know it, bedtime is about homework rather than simple enjoyment and fun. It can even transform into a point of conflict and something that children dread – it becomes something that causes arguments rather than something that binds parent and child together.

Although it took our species roughly 2,000 years to make the cognitive breakthroughs necessary to learn to read with an alphabet, today our children have to reach those same insights about print in roughly 2,000 days.

from *Proust and the Squid* by Maryanne Wolf

Over the years, I have talked to lots and lots of teachers about the transition into school. They highlight two aspects of this change. The first is that parents and teachers need to work together to reinforce the habit of reading for pleasure while the child is learning to read – it is very much a collaboration. The second is that the focus should be on enjoyment of reading at home, not on attainment – leave that aspect to the schools.

In fact, the majority of teachers regret the fact that schools need to concentrate almost entirely on the mechanics of reading. The curriculum has a big focus on testing and measuring children's skills, time is very tight, the timetable is packed and many teachers say that they simply do not have enough time to relax and read a story for the sake of pure enjoyment – with no agenda to test comprehension, for example. You can see how this situation sends out a message that reading is about learning more than anything else.

EXPERT VIEW

The school and the nursery will be encouraging the development of phonemic awareness and early letter sound connections. However, it shouldn't stop parents helping with reading development. If a child comes home from nursery and asks, 'What's that word, Mummy?' or 'How many sounds in this word?', the parent shouldn't feel that they shouldn't answer those questions.

David Reedy

As a parent, it is easy to be unsure of your role with reading when your child's world changes so dramatically when they start school. I have had parents ask me if they should stop reading to their children, or if they are really able to help their child with school reading because they themselves didn't learn phonics – and anyway don't understand them. Parents think 'Maybe it's best to leave it all to the school – leave it to the experts?'. If you do this, you are taking away a hugely pleasurable experience from your child, denying them (and yourself) wonderful bonding time, and above all, giving them negative messages about reading.

My answer to the question is that you should absolutely carry on reading with your child. The good news is that you get to do the fun bit of showing your child the joy of reading. An impressive 95 per cent of teachers view parents as the biggest influence on children's reading for pleasure, and they unanimously agree that parents and schools need to work together to encourage children to become enthusiastic readers. So keep reading!

The Reading Habit

Reinforcing the reading habit becomes more and more important as your child grows up. At the pre-school stage you were your child's entire world and beyond question the main influence. School moves your child away from you and into another bigger world – although you are still very much the centre of it! In this new world, outside influences begin to encroach from different angles: school, teachers, new friends, and new things to do, to explore and to enjoy.

Having a reading habit at home provides security for your child going out into this big new world. Home is a place they can return to and be reassured that the old world still exists with all its comforts and certainty. School, after all, can be bewildering. Trying to socialise with new people is hard, and it is stressful trying to understand and fit in with new rules and routines in a new environment. Knowing that home routines carry on as before gives reassurance. It provides a place where they don't have to worry about learning and taking on new challenges.

> **EXPERT VIEW**
>
> The reading habit is beneficial to children's emotional development, as well as sustaining a love of reading. During periods of change children often seem to regress so don't worry if they choose books that seem too young for them – everyone needs a bit of comfort fodder now and again.
>
> *Dr Amanda Gummer, child development expert*

The reading habit and routine you maintain at home can become an anchor and security for them. I remember in the early days that Louis really didn't want to go to school. One of the things I used to do on the way to school, both to distract and reassure him, was to talk about a favourite book and to say how much I was looking forward to reading it again at bedtime.

I asked a group of 250 UK primary school teachers to think about the following question: What would make the biggest difference to getting children to read for pleasure? Here are some of their responses.

Being given dedicated time during the school day and well-stocked school libraries.

The public attitude is that teachers are supposed to do everything, and the parents' input is not as important, but parents play an essential role and there is only so much teachers can cover in the classroom.

More space in the school day for whole class reading, paired reading and so on. Much of the reading in school is because we/they have to rather than for pleasure.

Seeing their parents read themselves for pleasure. Listening to their parents read aloud to them just for the pleasure of sharing a book. Teachers having a chance to read a class book to the children without having to do work about it!

Storytelling — they LOVE hearing stories and just don't get enough of this!

More time to share a variety of books in the classroom, with no 'agenda' — just reading together!

Schools giving workshops on the importance of encouraging your child to read.

Parents seeing how reading is key to their child's future success; they should read frequently with their child as well as discuss books and stories.

Make it okay to begin enjoying independent reading later in childhood.

Teachers reading a wide range of books to children and modelling good reading habits: for example reading when the children are reading in the library or silent reading times. Parents reading stories with/to their children more often.

Regular visits from authors/ professional writers to inspire the children.

More parental involvement.

Give more time to reading aloud, both stories and poems.

Spend time getting to know the child and what type of book may engage them.

By sticking to the reading habit you are sending your child a message that reading is an important part of your family's life. By doing that it establishes an assumption and acceptance – this is how it is in our family – it's part of our family's identity.

Children who were read to regularly by their parents at age 5 performed better in all three tests at age 16 than those who were not helped in this way.

Institute of Education study, September 2013

So how do you reinforce or establish the reading for pleasure habit when your child is struggling with decoding and phonics and all the changes going on at school?

📖 Make a reading commitment

One of the simplest things to do is to commit to reading to or with your child every day. Of course, some days it won't happen – the reality of our imperfect lives means that a severe lack of time, stress or childcare arrangements will get in the way. But you can create a haven of togetherness by committing to a reading routine – particularly if you fix it in your mind that it is the last thing you abandon on those impossible days, you'll usually find a space to read together.

If you have a time set aside from the pre-school years, maintain it. You might need to adapt a bit: so perhaps you'll have to cut four books a night down to three. Or you might have different times of day for different things. If you don't work, why not think about trying to find ten minutes straight after school? Sit down somewhere together, have a hug and something to eat, and share a book. Make it part of the end of school/beginning of home routine – you will enjoy it as much as they do! Bedtimes are the other obvious point in the day but sometimes time can be pressing even then. If it is, just explain to your child that you are so busy now that you can only read one book, but at the weekend there will be time for loads of books. Then make reading a highlight of the weekend.

Make a promise to yourself to read with them for a minimum of, say, ten minutes a day but try to do more. It really works.

📖 Learning to read is not reading for pleasure

Keep the homework reading or school reading scheme books separate from your reading for pleasure time. Make sure you clearly distinguish them in your child's mind: 'Do your school reading now and then we'll have a story later on.' Make bedtime (if that's the only time you have for reading for pleasure) story time, and read the school book at breakfast, when they get in from school or even on the bus in the morning. Never do school reading at bedtime. It's probably the worst time of the day for you and your child, and can easily lead to fractious and unhappy children (and parents!).

Beware also of concerning yourself with how your child's reading is progressing in comparison to other children. One mum of a 5 year old I talked to confessed that she could not help looking in the book bags of the children who came home to tea because she wanted to know what reading level they were on. This anxiety and competitiveness communicates itself to your child and is not helpful! Your child will learn to read fluently when they are ready to. Better to have a later learner who loves it than an early achiever who does not enjoy reading.

It is important to remember that there is no such thing as a typical child and learning to read at different ages is normal. One Year 3 teacher told me that in her experience it's perfectly normal in her class for some children to still be on the school reading scheme books, some to be on early chapter books such as *Horrid Henry*, while others are on *Harry Potter* or *Artemis Fowl*.

One parent of a 5 year old told me recently that when her daughter started school she pretty much gave up reading to her, but on advice she then reintroduced bedtime reading:

> It made me fall back in love with reading. It made me realise how important it is for giving us time together. I realise I must do it every day. I am now trying to do between 10 minutes and 45 minutes every day. Last night was tricky but we did it. She is now on chapter books so she reads a chapter of it to me and I read her a story too.
>
> *Emily, mum to Stella, age 6*

📖 Encourage them all the time

As they get it, and they eventually will, you will reach the point where they can read independently. But don't fall into the trap of thinking that just because they can read, they will read voluntarily. Many love reading at this point, they read fluently and enjoy the novelty of being able to do it alone. That is such wonderful thing. Some may be capable of reading independently but are reluctant to do so. However, for both types of readers, beware leaving them to do their own thing. Whatever you do, don't stop playing your part – reading to and with your child. So many parents think their children are reading independently means that they can forget about it. It is not like riding a bike, so don't take away your steadying hand too soon!

Why should you stay involved? Because today's environment is full of distractions and entertainment that are more immediate than reading. Once they have acquired the reading skill it doesn't mean they'll keep on using it for pleasure. Even if your child is keen right now, I can assure you as they become more exposed to peer pressure and the digital world, smart phones, apps, consoles and gaming will attract their attention. At a loose end, they will turn on the TV, or pick up the iPad or phone or whatever else comes to hand rather than a book. Of course there is nothing wrong with that – but you need to strike a balance.

Monitor screen time but don't make reading the enemy by banning all technology in its favour. Remember that reading is nothing more than a habit – a bit like brushing your teeth, but much more enjoyable! The more you practise it, the more chance it has to last a lifetime.

📖 Pack a book wherever you go

Let your child choose a book to slip into their backpack (along with whatever snacks they prefer) whenever you go on an outing. It'll help reinforce the idea of books and reading as an exciting part of their life.

Tablet use doubled in one year in this age group. 34 per cent of children now have access to a tablet computer – up from 17 per cent last year. This is also the age where gaming on smartphones peaks – 90 per cent of 5–7 year olds have access to and play games on a smartphone.

'The UK Children's Book Consumer in the Digital Age,' *Bowker 2013*

Boys and girls

Boys and girls are different. The effect of hormones is undeniable. The differences are inborn. For instance, testosterone compels boys to move in order to build their muscles, while girls find it easier to sit still. Girls tend to be more dextrous so they find it easier to hold a pencil and write. Their wrist bones are usually fully developed by the age of 4½, a full year before boys'. Boys' thumb muscles also develop later than girls', so it's more difficult to use the pincer grip for writing. Boys' fine motor skills are often delayed by up to a year and so they can find holding a pen or scissors extremely difficult. More generally, boys mature later than girls: by the age of 6 or 7, girls are socially, emotionally, cognitively, and even physically, 6–12 months more mature than boys.

On the other hand, the areas of the brain involved in targeting and spatial memory mature about four years earlier in boys than girls. This means that a two-year-old boy is about three times more likely than a two-year-old girl to be able to build a bridge out of wooden blocks. However, this kind of ability is perhaps less noticed in the classroom, where value tends to be placed on sitting still and concentrating.

So, you can see why the skills required in formal schooling can be hard for some boys to achieve. Boys can subtly be made to feel inferior because their bodies are not yet developed to deal successfully with what school is teaching, testing and measuring in these early years. They can quite easily feel they are not achieving. I remember one weekend when Louis, aged about five, was colouring. He became very cross with himself because he was going over the lines. He threw the pencil across the room shouting 'I can't do it and all the girls can.'

As if these inherent differences between boys and girls are not enough, our society makes more of them. The different hormones are innate, but social expectations are learned. There are stereotypes that we are all familiar with – boys are associated with being big and strong, noisy, active, the colour blue and not being able to sit still long enough to read. Girls are sparkly and fluffy, like to be princesses and fairies, are associated with the colour pink, being calmer and better able to concentrate on reading.

Yes, boys and girls are different but this just means they are not the same. It doesn't mean they are better or worse than each other. Whatever the differences, they should not be a reason to deny a boy the pleasure and lifelong benefits of reading. Yet this does happen. I have often heard parents make comments about their son's lack of interest in reading, and often the comments are voiced in front of the boy. One mum said to me 'He doesn't want to read, he's a boy, what do you expect?' while her five year old was sitting right next to her. This of course gives permission to the boy not to read – it becomes a self-fulfilling prophecy.

EXPERT VIEW

Girls are often praised for sitting quietly and reading and they get more positive reinforcement for being 'good readers' than boys who are traditionally expected to be more active. This leaves boys with little motivation to persevere with reading challenging texts, so the problem becomes exacerbated. This results in boys defining themselves as not being good at reading. The higher incidence of dyslexia in boys also compounds this.

Dr Amanda Gummer

It's very interesting to see differences in boys' media preferences from this young age. A 2013 Ofcom survey looked at the media activity children say they would most miss. For 5–7 year olds, top of the list was TV (57 per cent). But the activity where the gender difference is clearly marked is the playing of computer games: 28 per cent of boys, as opposed to 12 per cent of girls, would miss gaming most. Whether this is because they are given access to computer games more readily, because they are naturally drawn to it, or because it is socially the norm for boys, they tend to be into gaming at a younger age than girls and play much more intensely. Perhaps this reflects another gender difference: that boys' eye structures are more attuned to motion and direction, which is why they have better spatial visualisation and memory – another key physical difference that is not necessarily an advantage in the early school years.

Why am I sharing this with you? Why the spotlight on boys? The answer is that at this very early age, boys can become disenfranchised from both school and reading. It's crucial that your son associates reading with pleasure, that he enjoys being read to and reading. It will make him feel valued and increase his self-esteem.

New routines

Once your child has got used to going to school and is in a calmer frame of mind, try to find regular moments when you can settle down with a book. If both parents are working or you are a single parent and have only got time for a bedtime story, don't despair, just make it a regular event. Schedule a time every weekend for a story or two – and try to make it a special time, a time your child looks forward to. One family I know encouraged their six year old by setting half an hour aside each weekend when all of them read their books. Mum, dad, the six year old – and their two year old too, looking at his picture book about diggers.

If you are the father of a son it is really important to spend time reading when you can – children need role models and boys need male role models. Your son's school life is likely to be dominated by women (the vast majority of primary school teachers and carers are women) so spending time reading with them is vital.

EXPERT VIEW

The most crucial thing for dads to understand is that if kids see their dads reading they're more likely to enjoy it themselves. There is evidence that boys are slipping further behind girls in reading – and this emphasises how important it is that dads are positive role models to their sons as well as their daughters when it comes to reading.

Viv Bird, Booktrust Chief Executive

My father reading to me and my sister is one of my very first memories. I don't think without him reading every evening before we went to sleep either of us would be the people we are today. Everyone in my family reads at an alarming rate. It was the most natural thing in the world to go from listening to reading over my father's shoulder, to sneaking peaks at the book myself before he came to read to us, to reading to myself. My father worked long hours but we knew that that time was for us, even if it was the only time of the day we saw him, which made it special. I still remember the voices he did when reading the William books....

John Heaser, booktrust.org.uk

Playing catch-up

If you and your child have not yet got the reading habit, don't worry – it's never too late to start reading together. If you are just starting to set up a reading routine, the best way is to introduce the idea with a bit of lead time. Perhaps identify a particular date (start of term, half-term or a special occasion such as a birthday or going on holiday) so that you can build anticipation and start to pick out books you might want to read together.

Getting and maintaining the reading habit when your child starts school is crucial to establishing the reading habit for future years. And remember this isn't just about learning to read – this is about getting the reading for pleasure habit.

Reading for pleasure is more important for academic success than the family's socio-economic status.

OECD report, 2002

How to read

At school, the teachers are helping your child to learn the skill of reading. At home you are helping your child to love reading. You need to ensure you keep to your reading routine, and also that you create the right environment for it and make it as much fun as you can! You want your child to really look forward to your reading time together.

📖 The right environment

Creating the right environment, quiet time, is one of the most challenging things to do. Children's lives are full of hustle and bustle: getting ready for school, coming home tired and often wired, friends coming to tea, play dates, after school clubs. At home there are phones, tablets and other gaming devices at their fingertips. And it's not just the children: if you're working, your phone is probably pinging constantly with texts or emails long after the office has officially closed for the day! Time is relentlessly filled with distractions from so many angles that periods of time when we can all be still and quiet are getting rarer and rarer.

If you want your child to read, they need quiet time where they can concentrate and immerse themselves in a story. However, I have seen so many children who, when at a loose end, pick up something digital instead of picking up a book or a magazine. If you want your child to read you need to carve out this quiet time where reading can take root.

How do you do this? The easiest way is to restrict screen time. Switch off all devices for half an hour and get comfortable with a book. One mother told me: 'I do feel guilty sometimes because she might be eating her supper and I am on the computer. So I turn off all devices and we cuddle up on the sofa or on the big bed and read and she loves it. She loves the mummy time, I think. She loves my undivided attention. No other influences. And I want her to do this for her own children.' This is a good strategy. Provide all the comfort and security you can and, as much for your sake as your child's, turn off the distracting screens. If work emails or a friend texts, ignore it until you've had your uninterrupted reading time with your child.

As the children get older, screen time can get difficult to police so make your own family rules about it. Children, after all, like boundaries! They kick against them but deep inside they like to know what the rules are and like it when they are fairly enforced. Why not, for example, say yes to the Wii, Playstation and iPad only at weekends? One mother told me that her son is both a keen reader and gamer. They have got two simple rules: there are no screens in his bedroom (including phones) and he has a regular bedtime reading routine. This has been enough to ensure that he continues to enjoy his reading. If these ideas don't quite work for your family, find a different rule but stick to it. For more information about screen time see pages 18–31.

📖 Reinforce the magic of story

Take the opportunity when you are enjoying your book together (at bedtime for example) to reinforce the fun and enjoyment. Keep in mind all the time that the goal is to instil in them a lifelong love of reading.

You can both have great fun by choosing a character and then substituting your child's name. They love the thrill of being 'in the story'. I used to do this with *Cops and Robbers* by Janet and Allan Ahlberg – Office Pugh became Officer Louis. I sometimes stumbled over the words and had to change Pugh to Louis at the last minute – often we had a PughLouis! – but he didn't mind at all. Children are very forgiving, and you don't have to be perfect at it. He loved being in the story and being able to 'do things' as he saw it. Again, children are very restricted in what they can do in real life and he used to love pretending that he actually could, say, catch a robber.

Bring stories to life in the real world if you can. If you're reading a book such as *Shouty Arthur* you could take a camera or a notebook and look for wildlife, like the main character, Arthur.

Get your child to read to you by pretending that you are tired and want a break, then sit down with a cup of tea and carry out the role reversal by saying, 'I really enjoy it when you read to me'. Children love pretending to be the parent!

You can make or buy book plates for your children's books and get them to write their names in them. This introduces a great sense of ownership. The book becomes something even more valuable in their minds.

📖 Help build their attention span

When children start school their attention span starts to get stretched. There are two types of attention: focused attention is a short-term response to stimulus and it's very brief – perhaps lasting for eight seconds; heavy screen consumption reinforces this kind of short-term attention. Your child needs to build up the second type: sustained attention, which lasts typically 20 minutes (although in this mode we can refocus repeatedly so it's not all in one unbroken stretch). This kind of attention is what enables us to follow a lesson at school, watch a film or read a book. To help build this sustained attention, try stopping during a story and asking them what they think might happen next, or why a character did something. It keeps their attention and engagement.

📖 Praise any independent reading steps

As your child becomes more competent at reading for themselves they might want to show you how they can recognise words and read themselves. So, while you are reading a picture book, say 'Can you read that word/sentence?' Follow any efforts with 'Well done!' Use lots of positive language and praise them. Say, 'We'll tell Mum later that you read that!', 'Maybe you can read that again later when Mum's here!' or

'Let's phone Grannie and Grandpa and tell them – they'll be so pleased!'

📖 Vary the voices

If you are a working parent, and you can get home in time, see bedtime reading as a chance to have time with your child and hear about their day at school: what better way could there be to unwind, after all? If not, make it a weekend thing that you promise to do with your child if your spouse or partner is doing the weekday bedtime reading; even if you are not the main carer you can play a really special part. Ask grandparents, aunts, uncles – anyone with a known, trusted and safe voice. This is a great way to show how much reading is valued by your extended family and reinforces the idea of reading as a fun thing to do.

📖 Manage your time

If time is really tight and you are trying to squeeze in a story with your children, you can combine reading time by getting each child to choose one book and have them listen to each other's choice while you read. Sometimes encourage the older one to read to the younger if that's possible, and have the younger one listen to the older child's chosen book.

📖 Reinforce the story

There are a lot of really great book apps out there and, if used wisely, they can really help bring stories to life. There's just one golden rule: don't use them in isolation. If your child is having some screen time, let them play with book apps and then read the book again together later. All the time you should be encouraging them, reinforcing the idea that reading and stories are wonderful.

📖 Explore new genres and formats

If they are reading independently, encourage them, feed them new books, give them variety, and keep talking to them about what they are reading. And keep on reading to them too. If your child is reading well and confidently, try co-reading (see pages 102–3). This is where you share the same book and you take portions of the text in turn. Try reading a couple of pages to your child, then give them the book to read a page or two to you. This way you can expose them to stories that they might not try alone. A variation on this was shown to me by one family I know who have a six year old daughter. She's reading a book of short stories and their routine is that her mum or dad reads one of the stories, then she reads the next one.

One mother whose daughter showed no interest in independent reading told me that the school books turned her off and she wasn't excited by the choice on offer at home. However, a neighbour's daughter gave her the Enid Blyton Amelia Jane books. The following evening the mother went to check on her daughter who'd been very quiet, only to find her stretched out on her bed 53 pages into the book!

All of these tips and tactics will help keep their interest in, and love of, reading during the transition to school and the early school years – and they will also provide a whole host of shared memories and stories.

What to read

During these first years at school your child will progress through a school reading programme until they are able to read independently. At home and school they will graduate from picture books to chapter books – a big deal for children!

Chapter books feel so grown up, but they can carry with them a sense of disappointment because there are fewer or no wonderful pictures to accompany the story. Look for chapter books with illustrations to compensate for this. A great favourite in my house at this time was *Paddle-to-the-Sea* by Holling Clancy Holling.

> **EXPERT VIEW**
>
> Research reports a link between library use and reading for pleasure; young people that use their public library are nearly twice as likely to be reading outside of class every day.
>
> *(Clark and Hawkins, 2011) www.eriding.net*

As with anything for a child of this age, exploring what she likes and dislikes is half the fun. All reading is good reading – if your child is struggling with chapter books, look out for magazines or comic books such as *Asterix* or *Tintin*. Stories, non-fiction, plain fact books, magazines, comics – there's such a mass of reading material out there that you will always find something that suits and excites. A primary school teacher I know said, 'There's the right type of book for every child – it's just having the time to expose the children to all the different genres and letting them read in order to establish a liking for them!'

An essential part of this process is for the child to be able to start to make choices about what they like and dislike; as a parent you should absolutely be open to talk about this – if your child is finding a book boring, they should feel under no pressure to persevere. Give them permission to say they'd prefer to read something else – that way they feel more in control and reading for pleasure remains exactly that.

Many parents I talk to worry that their child sometimes wants to go back to reading picture books or books way below their reading age. The parents think that they're taking a huge step backwards and they push back against the child's love of these pre-school books. Don't! Learning to read is a difficult and tiring process; and going to school can be stressful. Let them revert to being a younger child if they need to. By re-reading these pre-school favourites you're reminding them of the closeness and security of those times and giving them the strength and confidence to push on and progress.

> **EXPERT VIEW**
>
> 'Comfort reading' is a valuable part of a love of reading generally. Everyone has different moods and when we're on top form it's exciting and interesting to challenge ourselves to try new things. However, when we're tired, ill or stressed, we revert to our comfort zone for reassurance and security. Don't prevent children from reading 'younger' books. In their own time, these books will become less appealing and the child will be ready to take on a new challenge.
>
> *Dr Amanda Gummer*

If your child is finding the transition to chapter books daunting, another strategy is to pick out books that are printed in a larger type size and have more space between the lines. The dense type in some chapter books (particularly when you get whole series bound up in one volume) can be very off-putting for the newly independent reader.

Other children (because they are all different!) will love

the big bind-ups. One girl of six I know was struggling to find something that she enjoyed and was given the *My Naughty Little Sister Collection* by Dorothy Edwards. She absolutely loved ploughing through all 752 pages of it.

Audio books are a great way to share stories on a long car journey or at home. Try sitting down at the weekend and listening together. Enjoy being read to by someone else!

Books that they can relate to are a good idea. First experience books are still valuable at this age. For example, *Mummy Laid an Egg!* by Babette Cole if there is a new sibling, or *Topsy and Tim Have Itchy Heads* by Jean and Gareth Adamson when the dreaded head lice strike!

With Louis we explored lots of different kinds of books and his interest in subjects changed over time. For a while he was really into nature books – the great thing about them is you can talk about the subject when you're out and about and then pick the books up again later when you get home. We worked through many factual books – the entire series of *Read and Wonder* for example. When he moved on to chapter books he tended to go for series. When he'd finished one, it was exciting for him to know that there were more to be read.

> **EXPERT VIEW**
>
> When books are challenging, series of books provide a familiar framework so that a child can direct his/her attention towards the story and vocabulary, and not have to learn new characters or writing styles at the same time. Reading the first in a series of books together and then encouraging a child to read the rest of the series him/herself is a great way of introducing new books and genres.
>
> *Dr Amanda Gummer*

When Louis began to read chapter books I noticed that he really missed the detailed illustrations he'd become used to in picture books. An early favourite was *Secret Agent Jack Stalwart: the Search for the Sunken Treasure: Australia* by Elizabeth Singer Hunt. This had some line drawings in it but they were few and far between. I remember he asked me if he could colour them in – 'adding detail' is actually how he put it! I know a lot of people would disapprove of this, but I could see he was missing the extra interest that the colourful pictures provided, so I allowed him to do it. He really enjoyed listening to the story and looking at his own pictures because it gave him a sense of ownership. It led to him making his own books. Anything you can do to ease the transition from picture books to chapter books is worthwhile – even if it means doing something generally frowned upon.

At this age your child will probably be trying to assert her own opinions more so get her involved in choosing the books she wants to read as well as picking things yourself. Don't be offended if the book you loved as a child and want to share is rejected. It's not personal!

<table>
<tr><td>EXPERT VIEW</td><td>Children love series. They like to read all the books in the series and collect them. They then do lots of other 'reading' things with them, sort them into order, favourites, re-read, recommend them to their friends, and so on. All of these are so important in developing as a rounded, engaged reader.

David Reedy</td></tr>
</table>

Children love their own popular culture and very likely will still be into certain characters. As with the pre-school years, they connect with characters at a fundamental level, which goes some way to explaining why they become so obsessed with them. You will always be able to find books and magazines about the characters they love, so use them to increase your child's engagement and enjoyment.

The Reading Home

Your job is also to keep getting in new books and magazines, a stimulating and varied supply. You should continue to encourage your children and enjoy discovering new things together. There are so many books out there and they can be found in so many different places: libraries, charity shops, book shops, online, in catalogues, at car boot sales, local and school fetes. Scour your local area for places where books can be found and encourage your children to come on a book hunt with you. Talk to the parents of their school friends about having a book swap after school one day a month, or ask the teacher if you can organise one in school.

Look out for local festivals and author events – these are becoming increasingly common as publishers and authors realise that direct contact with readers (young and old) is essential for getting their stories read. Libraries, schools and bookshops all invite authors to visit. If your child's school hasn't asked an author to come to see you, why not suggest it to the teacher?

Unavoidably at this age, technology will start to play a greater part in your child's life. The tempting shiny iPad, smartphone or laptop is a constant source of distraction for every child. There is nothing wrong with them using any of these devices and it would be unfair (and probably impossible!) to try to ban their use entirely. Use them to help: there are lots of places on the web and apps in the App Store where you can find great stories and ways to back up reading habits. Ask the teacher for recommendations and use them at home to encourage the exploration of different kinds of stories.

Another way of reinforcing reading is to make it a part of play dates. When your child's friends come over to play, set aside some time for a story. This will embed the idea that 'Ours is a reading home. This is how we do things.'

The Reading Home will evolve – in some ways as your child gets older the reach of the Reading Home extends into more aspects of their life. By going to events, swapping books with friends, going to the library and other reading-related activities your child's engagement with story becomes stronger, but at the heart of the connection is you and the home.

The transition to school and the acquisition of the skill of reading are challenges for any child. Help them not only to make the change but in the process maintain their love of story and reading by adopting some (or all!) of these strategies.

Dos and Don'ts

Dos

- ✓ Keep homework reading separate from story time or reading together.
- ✓ Try different places to practise school reading – on the bus, at breakfast, after school – but keep it separate from the bedtime story.
- ✓ Make a reading commitment to your child and establish a routine they can rely on.
- ✓ Set up a reading routine that fits in with the new life at school.
- ✓ Get other family members involved – spouse, siblings, aunties, uncles, grandparents.
- ✓ Look for books with illustrations if you feel your child is missing them.
- ✓ Be aware of the characters they and their new school friends are into – character books are great to have in your repertoire of stories. The characters are immediately recognisable and there are often a whole series of books so your child will be able to identify the next thing to read straight after finishing one.
- ✓ Introduce your child to book events and festivals from time to time.
- ✓ This is the time of the maximum number of parties, so give and ask to receive books! Buy sets from book clubs and split them up. It's a very cheap way to buy ten presents! Stockpile them for classmates' birthdays. It sends the message that books are desirable.
- ✓ Establish a rule about using screens and technology early on … and stick to it!

✓ Allow your child to revisit favourite pre-school books – development is never a smooth progression.

✓ Explore every avenue you can think of to find new and different things to read. Listen to what your child is interested in – respond to any clues about subjects that are of interest and seek out books or magazines about them. There's a book out there for everyone!

✓ Work with the school to encourage reading. Ask the school if they will be getting in authors to talk to the class.

✓ Have fun with events such as World Book Day – help your child work out how to dress up as her favourite character.

✓ Use apps and screens wisely. Book apps and websites can be great but make sure that they lead back to the physical book.

✓ Listen to an audiobook on long car or train journeys.

✓ Relate events in books to real life – if you're reading a book such as *Mr Wolf's Pancakes*, make some pancakes after you've read it!

Don'ts

✗ Don't use bedtime for homework reading – unless your child really loves the school book. Bedtime stories are about fun, comfort and relaxation.

✗ Don't assume that once your child is reading independently he will continue to read for pleasure unprompted, or does not want to be read to ever again!

✗ Don't be afraid to allow your child to personalise her books – a sense of ownership often encourages reading for pleasure.

✖ Don't ease up on the time you spend reading with your child. You need to be actively involved in the side of reading that isn't just about acquiring the skill.

✖ Don't be offended if the book you loved as a child and want to share with your child is rejected. It's not personal!

Q & A

What can I do? My child doesn't want to be read to any more.
Explore every different kind of subject matter and format. Allow him to choose the books and persevere! Find out the subjects he is really interested in and get any reading matter on that – a football magazine or story; a comic or fact book. It doesn't matter – just match the written material to the interest.

How do I keep up bedtime stories for more than one child?
The best way is to allow them to choose one story each for you to read with them individually and one that you can all read together. If you allow them both a choice and alternate which child chooses the book you read together, you should keep them both happy. Encourage the older one to help by reading some words or sentences depending on what stage they are at.

My child wants to read his old picture books rather than the books that are more appropriate for his reading age. Is this OK?
Don't worry – developmental progression is never smooth; often children need to take a step back before they can take another two steps forward. Allow him to choose the books that make him feel secure and confident. It's usually in preparation for making another developmental leap forward.

EXPERT VIEW

Piaget's explanation of development as assimilation and accommodation helps explain what's going on here. Children learn new skills/knowledge, but then their brains need time to make sense of it and fit it in with everything that's already in the brain. Keep reading more challenging books to him and with him and he'll eventually want to read them himself.

Dr Amanda Gummer

My child doesn't want to read independently. What can I do?
Don't be impatient. It can take longer to become an independent reader than you think. Keep reading to them and encouraging them, but don't apply any pressure.

Developmental Stages

These are some key developmental areas for 5–7 year olds.

READING
- Can name characters and setting in a drama, as well as act out real-life and imaginative situations through dramatic play.
- Can write some legible letters; begins to read independently but still enjoys being read to.
- Learns to read aloud.
- Enjoys making up and telling stories; knows a story has a beginning, middle and end.
- Begins to read a variety of literature for pleasure.

SOCIAL AND EMOTIONAL SKILLS
- Typically prefers structure and predictable routines.
- Begins to develop own interests and communicate preferences effectively.
- Increasing awareness of their own and others' emotions.
- Develops a more sophisticated sense of humour (and begins to move beyond slapstick).
- Enjoys sharing their writing with others.
- Instinctively helps other children when distressed; develops the ability to show sympathy; enjoys caring for pets.

THINKING SKILLS
- Role play and fantasy activities are typically very popular.
- Can find it difficult to make choices and do what

they're told when they don't understand.
- Begins to understand concepts of time and can learn to tell the time.
- Vocabulary rapidly increases as they enter formal education.

NOTE TO PARENTS: the speed of child development varies hugely from child to child and different skills are mastered at different ages – often determined by a child's environment. However, whatever age they acquire these skills, they are acquired in sequence, so children build up more complex skills on the foundations of previously mastered simpler skills. For example, a child cannot learn to write using fine motor skills until he or she has mastered the gross motor skills that underpin the muscle development. Above all, remember no two children are the same!

Chapter 4: Choosing to read

We shouldn't teach great books;
we should teach a love of reading.

B. F. Skinner, psychologist

At the age of 8, children are gaining confidence as readers. They have mastered the mechanics so most can now read quite well and can independently access stories, books and magazines appropriate to their ability. In a way, this is another beginning. The ability to read is the foundation on which to develop a real love of reading and to *become* a reader – someone who chooses to read for pleasure.

However, it is also the stage when many other things can distract children from reading. It's when your child feels that it is increasingly important to fit in with their group of friends and when those friends' opinions will often be repeated as if they are your child's own. Friends also have a big influence on what your child wants to do for hobbies and how they spend their free time. The digital world looms large in this: games, television and any other screen-based entertainment become the main playground currency. This really affects reading. Screens are very accessible and their use can easily become habitual. The extended time taken up by their use affects a child's ability to concentrate (as we saw in the last chapter) and eats up free time that could be used for reading. Screen use does have to be carefully controlled if you want to instil a love of reading in your child.

No entertainment is so cheap as reading, nor any pleasure so lasting.

Lady Mary Wortley Montagu, January 1753, giving advice to her daughter about the education of her granddaughter

Recent research shows that 37 per cent of 5–7 year olds rising to 62 per cent of 8–11 year olds go online almost every day. The change in mobile phone use between the two age groups is even more marked – rising from 8 per cent to 29 per cent.

'Children and Parents: Media Use and Attitudes', Ofcom, 2013

Because of these distractions, getting your child to the point of reading from choice will very likely take longer than you think. At this critical stage, your continued involvement and guidance is vital to give reading a chance to embed and become part of your child's life.

Children's tablet use is growing fast as more families buy them – use of tablets peaks at 8–10 years – currently at 45 per cent. It will grow as more and more families acquire them. Usage at 8–10 is higher than all other age groups.

'The UK Children's Book Consumer in the Digital Age', Bowker, 2013

The Reading Habit

By now you will have realised that parental involvement is essential to raising a reader! Your role when your child reaches this age is both to encourage independent reading and at the same time continue reading to, or with, them to reinforce the message that reading is a great joy and pleasure. Have a look at the graphs of children's activities opposite. You can see that this is a really pivotal time in a child's development because many parents ease off reading with their children, while the children's digital activities such as visiting YouTube and using mobile phones begin to grow.

The number of children in the UK who would rather use the internet than read a book is 32 per cent at 5–7, rising to 52 per cent at 8–11.

The UK Children's Book Consumer in the Digital Age', *Bowker, 2013*

If you look at early teens on the graphs, you will see how reading declines still further as the teens' focus switches to other activities. You need to take this as a warning sign. If you want your child to be a teenager and adult who loves to read, you must ensure that you don't ease off on embedding the reading habit now! By picking out the statistics you can see how reading drops dramatically in the teenage years – only 27 per cent of boys and 43 per cent of girls age 14–17 read to themselves weekly. So I hope you can see how important it is you stick with it at this age.

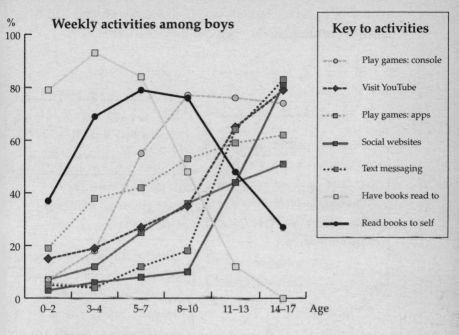

Weekly activities among boys

%

Key to activities

- Play games: console
- Visit YouTube
- Play games: apps
- Social websites
- Text messaging
- Have books read to
- Read books to self

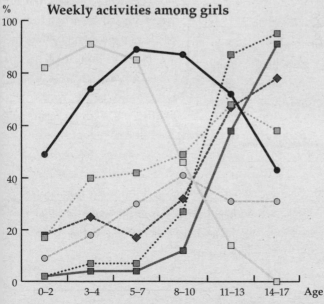

Weekly activities among girls

%

The UK Children's Book Consumer in the Digital Age', *Bowker, 2013*

I conducted a survey recently asking parents about their children's reading habits – here are some of the responses.

When we read together I realise how much they enjoy the time and how happy it makes us all feel. It also makes them want to read more on their own.

Mum about Jaril, age 7, and Ayisha, age 8

I wish he would read more. I should do something about it, shouldn't I?

Mum about Adam, age 9

Sami would rather be on the computer. He finds reading boring and he doesn't read unless I make him. But he does like it if I read to him to get it started then he finishes. He likes me reading to him, he wants me to do it a lot.

Mum about Sami, age 8

I've noticed my daughter will read something quite challenging, and then often revert to something easier afterwards.

Dad about Jemma, age 8

When I peep round the bedroom door at night and see her reading it makes me so very happy.

Mum about Amy, age 10

Homework and school reading has to be done. I feel under pressure and I think I have put her under pressure by making her finish books she doesn't like. I think I went a bit wrong. I've realised it's pleasure that will keep her reading independently, so it's okay to read things at a lower level than she is at if she enjoys it. Fun is the key, I think.

Dad about Tara, age 8

I don't really have trouble getting Kyle to read because I monitor the telly, laptop, time on the phone. He has a reading routine.

Mum about Kyle, age 9

At 8, my daughter is far too old to be read to any more!

Mum about Edie, age 8

My son doesn't like doing his school reading. He is more interested in factual books. Recently we got loads of books out and I read him a book I used to read over and over again when he was 4 — he became quite emotional about it.

Mum about Kerush, age 10

So why is it that many parents ease off reading? Well, from those I have talked to, it's clear that many parents think that because their child can read now, they will read. They expect and hope that their children will become independent and enthusiastic readers. Many parents also think that because their children can read they are now too old to be read to. One dad said to me of his nine year old, 'He's not a baby; he can read on his own. I wouldn't dream of reading to him at his age.'

I find this the saddest thing. There is nothing babyish about being read to. If you enjoy listening to an audio book in the car or a play or 'Book at Bedtime' on the radio, watching a great drama on TV or going to see a film, then you are enjoying a story and enjoying having it told to you.

Being read to is one of life's greatest pleasures. In ancient cultures, listening to stories provided fun, comfort and social glue. Language is what makes us human after all. Please don't think that reading to your child is only for the very young. Your older children will be missing out on some real magic and you will be holding them back.

📖 Keep the routine going

If your child has yet to really establish a reading habit of their own, keep encouraging them, keep the distractions at a distance, and create a quiet time and space for reading. Even if your child already reads from choice, keep your routine going. What looks like an established reading habit now can quickly fade without your involvement because of the myriad distractions on offer.

One parent spoke to me about her ten year old daughter, Chloe, 'She used to love reading but something's changed. Now I can't get her to pick up a book; all she wants to do is text her friends.'

📖 Have clear screen time rules

Clearly the digital world holds huge opportunities for our children and we want them to enjoy and benefit from it, but you need to get some balance in your child's life and ensure screen time does not take over. As I have said before, I have met lots of families where parents tell me they wish their child would read, but instead – and increasingly around this age – screen time is allowed almost 24/7. To make time for reading, clearly state the rules, stick to them and, alongside this, have a reading routine.

Due to peer pressure, your child will inevitably moan about this. You'll be told that their friends are allowed to do almost everything whenever they want to (play on the iPad in the evening, watch TV in their bedroom, spend all afternoon on the Xbox – I have heard it all!). You need to stick to your guns, knowing you are doing your child a huge favour in the long run. Explain that every house has different rules, there will be things we do differently to other families, and that that is what life is like.

Don't give in to emotional blackmail. One parent told me 'I remember Jay, age 11, coming home from school and saying, "In the jigsaw puzzle that is my school I am the only piece that doesn't fit because I am the ONLY boy who has not got *Call of Duty* and can't join in the conversations."' (For more information on screen time see pages 18–31.)

📖 Bedtime reading is essential

The bedtime reading routine continues to be a very important anchor in your child's life – it still provides comfort, relaxation and a quiet time, and it allows you both to enjoy a story.

This is the time when they can luxuriate in attention from either mum or dad (or both). This period together every day is invaluable for your child on an emotional level, and essential for your maintenance of a strong relationship with them. Peer pressure is being piled on thick and fast now and, coupled with all sorts of new anxieties at school – falling in and out with friends, sometimes feeling excluded – this produces complex emotions that children often find difficult to talk about.

If you are a busy working parent, finding time to try to help them deal with all of this is difficult. A bedtime story routine can provide exactly what you need. You may find your child starts to talk to you about things that are bothering them and it will give you the opportunity to reassure and guide. Reading together is such a positive, warm thing to do and creates feelings of safety and reassurance.

📖 Encourage independent reading

Many children can be reluctant to take the step to becoming independent, to reading alone. Even when they are able to do so, it can be daunting, they may be very tired from school and other activities, or they might simply not have got into the habit of reading for themselves. One strategy that really works in the encouragement of independent reading is to take advantage of the fact that children often want to stay up late. Try saying, 'It's time to turn the lights out and settle down, but if you want ten more minutes before we do that, you can read.' I can almost guarantee your child will go for it!

📖 Go looking for books

Making regular visits to bookshops and libraries, and rummaging in charity shops can help embed the reading habit. If you get the chance, introduce your child to book events such as author signings at local bookshops, or even better and a real family treat, go to one of the many literary festivals and listen to authors talk about their books and characters – this can be so inspiring.

At this stage Louis did judo and he loved everything to do with martial arts. On one occasion, I took him to see Chris Bradford, author of the *Young Samurai* series, at the Hay Festival in Wales. The audience was gripped as the author really brought the story and characters to life standing there dressed in Japanese robes and wielding a samurai sword! It was so impressive an image that I should think every child present wanted to read the book afterwards.

And book days at school are a good opportunity to get children interested in reading. Dressing up as their favourite character is a great way to reinforce the fun of it all.

Boys and girls

It's very important that you make no distinction between boys and girls when it comes to reading. Our society often seems to have lower expectations of boys and it's amazing how prevalent this view is. You might be surprised – or even horrified – at how often parents say to me of their sons, 'Boys don't like reading', 'Boys prefer gaming' and so on. It seems to be such an accepted thing that they will even say these things in front of their son.

If a boy hears this, imagine what it does to his reading commitment and to his opinion of himself? There is no reason why boys can't love reading. It is true that boys seem to be more attracted to gaming than girls are, but there is room in life for both!

EXPERT VIEW

Self-fulfilling prophesies can limit children's outcomes – a boy who thinks he is bad at reading will not challenge himself or read for pleasure, and so will find reading increasingly difficult. The trick is to find interesting subject matter. Getting gripped by a book is key and everyone who loves reading knows the thrill of being captivated by the story. Parents should worry less about what boys read – comics, football programmes and so on – rather, they should ensure that they are reading something, even if it's in a digital format, as this keeps the window of opportunity open for them to find a story book that will captivate them and lead them to reading for pleasure.

Dr Amanda Gummer, child development expert

The Reading Home

Life is busy! Life is noisy! To give reading a chance to take root and flourish you need to create the right environment for it. You might think this sounds odd if your memory of your own childhood is that time didn't seem to be an issue, and picking up a book now and then, maybe when you were at a loose end, was easy. But children's lives today are so different. They simply don't have moments when they are at a loss for something to do. They are busy with after-school activities and homework. Digital devices are at their fingertips and the time is easily filled. It is so simple for them to send a text, or play a game, play with an app, turn on the TV, go on social networking sites or explore YouTube – all of which are much more immediate than reading a book or magazine.

There are relatively low levels of phone ownership at 8 and under, but at 9 children's phone ownership begins to take off. 20 per cent of 9 year olds have a phone now, and it grows fast, so that by 11 when starting secondary school 62 per cent have a phone.

'Children and Parents: Media Use and Attitudes', Ofcom, 2013

To counteract this, your home should be full of a variety of reading matter – books, magazines and newspapers. If your child thinks e-reading is cool, then give it a try as it might be an incentive.

> The first thing I do after school is get a book out.
> My mum reads to me in bed every night.
>
> *Emily, age 10*

There should be no screens in the bedroom – TVs, DVD players, laptops, gaming consoles – and that includes phones. How are you going to get them to focus on reading if their phone keeps pinging with texts demanding to be answered? Some children's bedrooms are like media hubs! Parents I recently met told me that they wished their 11 year old would read more. When I saw the girl's room it was clear what the challenge was – she had a TV, stacks of DVDs on the bookshelf, a DS and a Wii in there. She also had a smartphone. It would take the most focused child in the world to ignore all that and pick up a book! Make sure your child has a bookshelf in their bedroom so that they can see their collection of books and view them as a source of entertainment.

As with younger children, it's still important to set an example and read in front of your children. Your child is getting to the stage where they may begin to challenge what you say, so it's best to adopt the approach 'do as I do', and not 'do as I say'! Try to spend some time reading your own book, magazine or newspaper at the weekend – grab half an hour and a cup of coffee and sit down with your child for some family reading time, each of you reading your own choice, side by side.

As well as showing that you like to read, show your child that you can spend time without a screen. Our lives are so hectic these days and we are often texting, answering work emails in the evening, ordering supermarket shopping online, updating Facebook and so on. You need to have time off-screen too, to show that doing other things is equally valid.

The Reading Home at this age is a more diverse concept than when the children were younger, when preferences for things they liked to read and spend time on were more fixed. As children get older they become more open to new things and so the opportunities to extend the Reading Home into bookshops, libraries, festivals and other book-related events grow. The outside world can enrich the Reading Home.

How to read

We have established that you need to both encourage independent reading and continue to read to your child. Co-reading can really come into its own at this point. Through this, your child will be able to appreciate books with content older than their reading ability might allow them to access. Co-reading is where you share a book and take it in turns to read aloud to each other. They read a page and you read a page, or they read a page or two and you continue to the end of the chapter. You can start with as little as a paragraph each and build it up over time. There's no rush, just take it at a comfortable pace for your child. Co-reading is a great way to introduce your child to books they might not otherwise tackle on their own because they may have seen them as too challenging.

The benefits of co-reading are easily summarised:

• **It helps children to access a lot of books**, speeding up the process because you can motor through the pages together.

• **It keeps their interest** because you are reading a wider variety of books together and ensuring they don't get bored.

• **If reading is laborious** for them, they can take ages getting to the point of the story and may give up too soon. Co-reading speeds up the process and they get involved more quickly.

• **It counteracts any problems** with concentration and attention spans. You are exposing them to the rewards of a good story and showing them that it's worth persevering.

• **It's a way of modelling reading**, giving an example, showing you enjoy it, showing them how to read aloud.

• **You can enjoy time together** – the best part for me was when it was Louis' turn to read aloud. I would shut my eyes and relax after a hard day – almost reverting to childhood myself. It's so lovely to be read to and it's heaven to be read to by your own child!

For the last couple of years our bedtime reading routine has been Marco reading a bit of the book I am reading to him — we've read things like *Harry Potter*, *The Little Grey Men* and so on. He reads a few pages then I take over. In this way he has become familiar with more challenging writing. After this he reads on his own for 15 minutes. He has typically chosen to read *Asterix*, joke books, *Tintin*, comics and so on. Even if he was really enjoying the book we were reading together he would not read it alone. But now, for the first time, he is choosing to read a novel. He is reading *Alice's Adventures in Wonderland*, which Granny gave him for his tenth birthday. I have already got *Through the Looking-Glass* and kept it to one side so he can carry on if he wants to!

Mum of Marco, age 10

If your child does not want to co-read, don't push it. Just make sure that alongside whatever reading they do, you keep on reading to them.

Use audiobooks to extend reading range

Audio books can be very useful at this stage. As with co-reading, you can introduce your child to books they might not be able to read themselves because they are above their reading level. You can also introduce new types of books and new genres. Importantly you can share them with your child, listening to them on a car journey, perhaps, and talking about them afterwards.

Find the time and the motivation

Life is busy and sometimes reading with your child can seem like yet another thing to do in an already overloaded day. It can easily slip and you need to be determined to stop this happening.

> In 2012, 53 per cent of parents of 8–10 year olds said they were reading less to their children than in the previous year.
>
> *'Children and Their Reading', YouGov, 2013*

My advice is to think of the time spent reading together positively. It really is not a chore. Think of it rather as a perfect time to be close to your child, and give yourself a pat on the back that you are making a good investment in their future – of more value than almost anything else you can think of. The National Literacy Trust says that, even at the age of 16, parental interest in a child's reading is the single greatest predictor of their achievement. And when you consider that 20 per cent of children leave primary school without being able to read at the expected level for their age, it's clear that your child needs you. As you build up the time reading together you will see how many benefits it gives your child and this will make you want to carry on.

EXPERT VIEW

Keeping an interest in books doesn't only mean reading aloud together, it is also about having conversations about what you both think of the story or text. After word reading skills have been achieved, reading progress is about deepening understanding, including the ability to read between the lines.

David Reedy, literacy expert

📖 Juggle your time

If you have more than one child and time is tight, compromise by trying to read a book or a chapter that is age-appropriate to each child. Let each of the children choose. If they sit and listen to their sibling's choice, so much the better.

Even if you can only manage ten minutes a night, do that every night. It's better to do little and often than long periods of nothing followed by a splurge at the weekend. However, I do know sometimes life gets in the way – we work late, things go wrong, we get ill, or we just cannot be around for whatever reason. If your routine slips every so often, so be it, but just keep going and consciously try to make time for reading with your child.

I can't claim to have read to my son every night. I've had to work late and occasionally I've even had an evening out! See if you can get someone else to read to your child if you can't – sometimes my husband takes over – or you can ask an older sibling or even the babysitter to do it. The point of the routine is that it is there. If from time to time it doesn't happen, the habit is there and will be picked up again the next time.

> It seems if you make a habit out of something it makes it easier to do!
>
> *Mum to Jason and Javina, ages 8 and 10*

If you are getting frustrated that your child's independent reading seems to be taking a long time to get going, try to remember that getting to a point where your child regularly and routinely chooses to read for pleasure is not a quick fix. You have made a commitment to help your child love reading and you are doing something wonderful for them – so valuable for their happiness, education, well-being, knowledge, and for your relationship with them. Feel good about it!

What to read

Anything and everything! This is the age when your child is discovering more about themselves, working out what they are really interested in and developing their own identity and character. You will need to supply lots of different books, magazines and articles for your child to try – and there is so much choice that this is easy to do. The trick is to strike a balance between you supplying and suggesting things, and encouraging your child to actively choose new reading material so they have a sense of personal choice, ownership and involvement.

You never know what will inspire them. Take your child to the book aisle in the supermarket, to the bookshop, to charity shops, to car boot sales; see if anything there catches their eye. Think about what they are interested in and what they have enjoyed reading so far, and seek out things you think might hook them in.

Look for books and magazines that reflect their enthusiasms and talents. For example, if your daughter loves to dance, try the book *Ballet Shoes* by Noel Streatfeild, or if your son responds to music and loves rhythm and rhyme try poems such as 'Cargoes' by John Masefield or 'Night Mail' by W. H. Auden; if they are especially fascinated by mysteries try the *Alex Rider* series. For more ideas see pages 13–15.

Collecting is a natural stage of development around this age, so you can capitalise on this by getting all the books of favourite authors, or buying a series of books. The great thing about a series is, of course, that it is so easy to keep the reading going because your child will want to read the next one. Louis would finish one of the Alex Rider books and ask for the next immediately.

88 per cent of girls and 71 per cent of boys 8–10 years old like collecting book series.

'The UK Children's Book Consumer in the Digital Age', Bowker, 2013

Children love their own popular culture. You may find a good magazine really hits the spot, with information feeding their emerging interests in films, gaming, pop music, art and craft, and football or other sports. If they love a magazine, get a subscription. If they're still exploring the choices, make it part of your family routine to go and choose one at the weekend. If you have a very sporty child, the sports pages of the newspaper can be a great thing to give them to read because it makes them feel very grown up! And other media can open up an interest in reading. If they have enjoyed watching a film, TV programme or DVD, give them the book and explain that the book always has more in it than the film so it will be even better! Good ones to try are *Stig of the Dump*, *Tracy Beaker*, *Harry Potter*, *War Horse*, *Tom's Midnight Garden* and *Tintin*. One dad recalled how he took his daughter on a Christmas theatre trip to see *Mary Poppins*. She loved it so much that when he told her there is a book the show is based on, she asked him to read the book to her.

Gaming can offer ways into reading too! The gaming companies that make *Minecraft*, *Moshi Monsters* and so on also publish books – if you have a dedicated *Minecraft* or *Skylanders* player, try one of the books. Even if you think this is not proper reading and you'd love your child to read a novel instead, don't fret. Remember, it's about enjoyment. If your child enjoys reading they should be receptive to reading more. It's a long journey and all sorts of material will be read on the way.

Humorous books become particularly interesting for boys and girls at age 8–10. Sharing a joke can be a great bond between you and your child as you delight in each other's laughter. It's like being in a club together. You can mention the subject at other times and you both just know. *You're a Bad Man, Mr Gum* by Andy Stanton was like that for Louis and me. For a long time after we had read the book, if Louis wanted to watch a TV programme, he'd say, 'Can I watch a bag of sticks?' (You'll have to read the book to understand!).

At 8–10 years of age, boys often show a strong interest in science and nature books, while girls can favour stories about children and families. But these are generalisations and variety is the key! Remember there is no such thing as a typical child – you might be surprised at what interests your son or daughter. At this age Louis loved *My Family and Other Animals* by Gerald Durrell – science, nature, families and children all rolled into one!

Children often really miss looking at illustrations, so look for books with pictures, or magazines, comic books or factual books that are illustrated. The huge success of books such as *Diary of a Wimpy Kid* and *The Dork Diaries* shows how much children love illustrations.

At 8–10 children's interest peaks in comic strip books/graphic novels (37 per cent) and annuals (53 per cent) as they move from picture books to text-based reading.

'The UK Children's Book Consumer in the Digital Age', Bowker, 2013

I talked about the increasing influence of children's friends at the beginning of this chapter. This influence can be great for reading! Ask your child what their friends are reading and see if they want to read it too.

At 8–10 years, 70 per cent of children say they like reading what their friends read…. 76 per cent of girls and 55 per cent of boys aged 8–10 say they recommend books to their friends.

'The UK Children's Book Consumer in the Digital Age', Bowker, 2013

Try suggesting books you liked as a child. They may reject them but they may well click. Louis used to say to me, 'You loved these books, didn't you?' when we read the *Swallows and Amazons* series together. This connection with your own past provides a sense of family tradition, security and belonging. And you can return to old favourites too, which might be very comforting to your child. One mum told me that her 11 year old daughter was made more anxious about the transition from primary to secondary school when she found out her best friend was going to go to a different school. She became very upset and unsettled. One bedtime her mum asked her what she'd like to read and she (rather embarrassed) asked for a really old favourite, *The Tale of the Flopsy Bunnies* by Beatrix Potter, and tried to make light of it by saying it was 'for old time's sake'. Her mum realised that the book was pure comfort for her.

Poetry can really click with children at this age. Poems are often quite short, accessible and therefore not off-putting. And, of course, the variety is immense. There are some amazing anthologies. Try *A Shame To Miss* poetry collection by Anne Fine. A collection called *Orange Silver Sausage* was Louis' great favourite. Children love to laugh, so funny and ridiculous poems and limericks can really connect with them. Try Roger McGough, Edward Lear, Hilaire Belloc's *Cautionary Verses*, Lewis Carroll and Spike Milligan. Try making up poems together, and then read some more to get further inspiration.

School

As your child progresses through school, you will probably have less contact with their teacher. Children go in to school on their own, and parents can usually only go as far as the school gates and not up to the classroom door. Even if it's hard to talk to the teacher in person, you can usually email them or write them a note and send it in with your child. I have always found teachers very willing to help and advise. They want your child to read for pleasure just as much as you do, and they can be a mine of information about books to try because they have so much experience and are full of ideas and knowledge. Also, they see how your child reacts to different subjects and can perhaps give you tips about a topic that has really engaged them. Maintaining a link with the teacher and what's going on at school is a bit more difficult but it's just as important as it was when children first start school. You, your child and the school will all benefit.

Homework increases as your child moves up through the school years and reading will have a focus – typically your child will be expected to read every day at home for 15 or 20 minutes, and some schools specify reading aloud. They may enjoy this, they may not. Reading aloud is not always easy. If they enjoy the book there is no reason for them not to read it at bedtime to you. But, as with younger children, if they really don't like it, try to get them to do it at another time – ideally when they are not too tired. You can also talk to your child's teacher and see if you can find other books that might interest your child more. Keep bedtime for indulging your child in the kind of books and stories that he really enjoys. By doing this, you will preserve the wonderful happy reading occasion together that you have been working so hard to build.

Children are supposed to read for 20 minutes each night out loud at our school and he hates it and I sometimes wonder if I should leave it. He loves *Wimpy Kid* though, and gets *Match* magazine too. If he was asked to read these for school, he'd be happy.

Mum about Jamie, age 10

As they get older they may have to read a set book that they are studying in class. If they don't like the book there is a danger that this will be seen as work and not fun. A good strategy for this is to co-read (see pages 102–3) the text book they are studying – you can help them get through it and probably make it more interesting for them if you can add in some emphasis, intonation and colour with your reading. It's also a good time to ask questions and help them learn a little more by stimulating their curiosity about the subject.

If you can give any of your time to volunteer at the school it will be so welcome. You might try to sign up to listen to children reading. Not only will you be doing a great thing, you will also be picking up hints and tips for your home reading and sending out a strong message to your child that reading is so important that you are helping the school with it. Try to encourage your school to get authors in to talk to the children – this is very exciting and inspiring.

This crucial stage in the development of a lifetime reader is all about making sure that the newly acquired skill of reading is used habitually for enjoyment. Just because your child can read, it doesn't mean that they will read. Linking the things they enjoy with books and reading, having a reading habit or routine, and creating a reading home where books, magazines and newspapers are easily accessible, as well as banning screens in the bedroom, are all great ways of ensuring success.

Dos and Don'ts

Dos

- ✓ Keep the reading routine going – stick with it and keep reading to your child.
- ✓ Restrict screen time.
- ✓ Have a 'no screens in the bedroom' rule.
- ✓ Ensure a wide variety of reading material is available.
- ✓ Look for other media adaptations of stories that can drive interest in reading – films, TV programmes, DVDs, gaming, theatre.
- ✓ Set an example and read your own book or magazine in front of your child.
- ✓ Set an example and make sure you have time offline when with your child.

Don'ts

- ✗ Never bring gender into it! Boys can be readers just as much as girls can.
- ✗ Don't expect too much too soon – independent reading may take longer than you think. Be patient.
- ✗ Don't ease off on your time reading with your child.
- ✗ Don't get frustrated if your child reads slowly. Better to read slowly and enjoy it than race through to get it over with!
- ✗ Don't show any disapproval of your child's choice of reading materials if you think they are not challenging enough. All reading is good reading, including comics, magazines, online comic strips, comic books and graphic novels.

Q & A

My daughter is so busy with homework and after school activities, there is either no time for reading or she is too tired. How can I get her to read?

Bedtime reading is the answer. Even it it's just for ten minutes, make it part of the daily routine and it will happen.

My 9 year old son is perfectly able to read for himself but shows no interest at all – he just wants me to read to him. How can I get him to read for himself?

Try focusing on co-reading. Get him to read just a page (or even just a paragraph) and then carry on with reading the story yourself. Gradually build up the amount that he reads aloud to you. This should get him into the habit of reading for himself.

My son is only interested in gaming and going on YouTube. I can't get him interested in anything else at all. How can I get him to read a book?

First you have to restrict screen time. You will need to find rules that suit your family – such as just at the weekends, or one hour a day only – whatever you feel is reasonable. Then you need to make sure the bedtime reading routine happens. In this way you are making a place for reading to happen, creating an environment where it can take root and grow.

My daughter doesn't seem very interested in books any more. The big attraction is texting her friends – to the exclusion of most other things. How do I get her interested in books again?

Try all sorts of reading material. You may find that magazine interest her, for example. All reading is good! Make sure she does not have her phone in her bedroom at night-time and persevere with offering a wide choice of reading materials. Something will click.

Developmental stages

These are key developmental areas for 8–11 year olds.

READING

- Begins to read complex stories for pleasure on own and is able to remember the plot over longer periods.
- Likes stories about famous people, adventures and mysteries.
- Enjoys both real life and fictional stories and can distinguish writing styles that go with each.
- Reads aloud more fluently and sometimes includes intonation and emphasis.
- Creates own engaging and detailed stories.
- Enjoys the responsibility of reading aloud to younger children.

SOCIAL AND EMOTIONAL SKILLS

- Knows that other families may be the same or different and feels a sense of security and comfort in own family setting, but can start to challenge accepted family rules.
- Peer pressure and a need to belong tend to be very important influences on behaviour.
- Can be very dramatic in responses and play.
- Starts to use accessories, such as clothes, toys, books, and allegiances, to express personality and develop

a sense of identity. (And so is more likely to read a 'cool' book or something that reflects the persona that the child wants to portray.)

- Develops a sense of empathy.

THINKING SKILLS

- Can distinguish between fantasy and reality but has a tendency to straddle the world between make-believe and reality.
- Can follow complex instructions and predict future outcomes.
- Is developing an understanding of hypothetical situations.

NOTE TO PARENTS: the speed of child development varies hugely from child to child and different skills are mastered at different ages – often determined by a child's environment. However, whatever age they acquire these skills, they are acquired in sequence, so children build up more complex skills on the foundations of previously mastered simpler skills. For example, a child cannot learn to write using fine motor skills until he or she has mastered the gross motor skills that underpin the muscle development. Above all, remember no two children are the same!

Chapter 5:
Staying connected

*Reading is to the mind what
exercise is to the body.*

Richard Steele in the *Tatler*, March 1710

The teenage years are generally viewed as challenging. There is so much change from the anxious child starting out at secondary school to the 16 year old who has just finished their GCSEs. Over these years, your teen will become less and less dependent on you – superficially at least. Part of growing up is, after all, about cutting the apron strings and striking out.

Your relationship with your child will change hugely over the same period. And although teens might like to think themselves grown up, they still really need your guidance but often just don't want to hear it! Teenagers can be rebellious and rude. They may lie to you, it can seem that they don't care about anything you think is important, and you can feel completely shut out of their lives. This is very hard to take when you have been the centre of their world for so long. For you as a parent this can be a difficult, stressful and upsetting time.

It might help to understand what is going on if you know that this transition is just as hard for them because this is a time of inner conflict. They are compelled to push for independence but might find this frightening. They want freedom but not responsibility. They have to deal with many body changes, can be very self-conscious, often feel misunderstood and have huge mood swings. They want to fit in with their peer group but need to find their individuality. There is a lot of pressure from schoolwork and exams, and there are big decisions to make about their future. In all this, they feel the weight of parents' expectations and anxieties. Although it might not seem like it, they really need you and your support, and they need unconditional love.

EXPERT VIEW

Communication is key to navigating these potentially stormy waters. It's much easier to communicate using a shared activity, so making time for things that you can enjoy together is hugely important.

Dr Amanda Gummer, child development expert

Amid all this turmoil, you might think how on earth is there going to be a place for reading? The good news is there can be. Even better, reading can actively help you both through these years. Reading can act as a bridge between your former pre-teenage life together and the more difficult present. Points of reference from shared stories will still appeal to your child's memory of the comfort and undivided attention they received from you in years past. In addition to the emotional support, teenagers really gain practically from reading as well.

I read to Maya from when she was tiny. I was still reading to Maya at 14 years old — she loved having the personal attention from me, instead of having to share me with her younger brother; it helped her go to sleep at night. Somehow, though, with her schoolwork and hobbies my reading to her stopped. And at 15 and 16 she read much less independently too, although she did read magazines every week. What her friends were into made a big impact. Films were a big motivation too. Gradually school demands made her less interested and reading for pleasure did take bit of a back seat. She's 19 now and has come back to reading more. I and her mum pass books on to her and we chat about them.

Steve, dad to Maya

So how will your teen benefit from reading? The short answer is 'in many ways'. Of course their schoolwork will be improved by reading widely around a subject. But more than that, reading is a relaxation, an escape from pressure and from boredom. It gives teens the ability to live vicariously and explore things in their imagination that they are too young to experience in real life.

Reading is also a great comfort during times of teen angst. Reading about other teens' experiences can help make your child feel that they are not alone, that others think like they do, and that they can find advice and guidance on things they might feel too awkward to talk about to their parents.

Reading together will also provide you with a tool to discuss issues that come up and fiction can provide a distance from the issues. That prevents them from being too personal – by discussing how characters feel and act, teens are able to develop insight and emotional intelligence that will stand them in good stead in later life.

Dr Amanda Gummer

Reading and reading together will be a great source of comfort and reassurance in these very difficult years. It will help maintain a link between you and your child and help them to discuss things with you. If you carry on sharing stories then there will always be some neutral ground to chat about – books you have both read. It will be a refuge for you both from everyday life, somewhere where there's no nagging or conflict!

The Reading Habit

Your teen might have less time for reading and less interest in it too. There are a lot of things going on that contribute to this. Peer pressure, concern with fitting in and preoccupation with what others think of them all play a part. Sadly, many teens think reading is not cool.

Also, the increasing amount of time teens spend using technology, their busy lives, the pressure of school work and an emergent social life, can erode reading time. Put simply, there never seems to be a quiet moment to be still and read because time is relentlessly filled.

A recent survey showed just how much reading suffers in secondary school and how uncool reading is perceived to be:

		Age 8–11 (school years 3, 4, 5, 6)	Age 12–14 (school years 7, 8, 9)	Age 15–16 (school years 10, 11)
I would be embarrassed if my friends saw me read	Boys	22%	25%	23%
	Girls	18%	23%	17%
Reading is cool	Boys	49%	28%	20%
	Girls	59%	32%	29%
I read outside of class every day	Boys	32%	21%	18%
	Girls	43%	28%	23%

National Literacy Trust report, 2013 survey

One of the big challenges over these years is keeping communication open, and as they get older, even just spending time together. There is a tendency for teens to shut themselves away – physically and emotionally – by closing their bedroom door and by offering little conversation. Friends are very important, and as they get older, boyfriends and girlfriends may appear on the scene, preoccupying your teen. By being involved with their reading you will still get some precious time together. And you will also experience a real closeness, the opportunity to talk and share opinions, and the chance to show them how much you love them. Reading has the power to connect at the deepest level, bringing comfort and delight. It is the 'relationship glue' that I have talked about a previous chapters.

Just as you need to adapt your approach to parenting with teenagers, you need to adapt your approach to how you encourage a love of reading. You'll need to acknowledge their increasing maturity by adopting different strategies. What is good for a 12 year old may not work with a 16 year old. And children develop at different rates and have different personalities. Your 15 year old daughter may be a home-bird, or she may be a sociable extrovert with a boyfriend who 'treats the house like hotel!'.

EXPERT VIEW

Keeping reading going is just as important in the teenage years as at any other time. Parents/carers just have to be more subtle about their input, in order to encourage talk around, and enjoyment in, reading, while making it not look like they are demanding it should be done.

David Reedy, literacy expert

Whether you want to continue to encourage and reinforce your child's existing reading habit or reignite an interest, the most important thing is to be involved in whatever way you can, and in the most appropriate way for your teen. Don't step away! Create a connection between you and your child with reading as the bridge, allowing you to talk about books, share stories and do things together around books and writing.

The best situation you can be in is to arrive at these years with the foundations of a reading habit. You can then adapt your approach to accommodate the twists and turns of adolescence. But if you are almost starting out and still trying to make it tak root, don't despair because there are still things you can do.

Despite the challenges I have talked about, you will be pleased to know there are plenty of teenagers who love to read. I asked some 12–16 year olds from two London schools about their reading habits:

GIRLS

My mum loves reading and she makes sure me and my sisters read at least half an hour every single day.

Fatma, age 12

I got my reading habit from watching movies which had books and then reading the book. I'm reading the *Noughts and Crosses* series now.

Beth, age 13

I read a really good book that I thoroughly enjoyed and since then I have started reading a wider variety of books on a regular basis.

Jasmine, age 14

I enjoy reading a lot, anywhere, anytime. I have a reading habit and I got it from being drawn into books. I have around 100 books in my room. My parents do still read to me sometimes. We have a rule that I am not allowed my mobile phone upstairs. I'm reading *Cross My Heart and Hope to Live*.

Alice, age 13

My parents make me read fc half an hour before I sleep. I ca get engrossed in a really goo book in seconds. I can only hav an hour of screen time a day. I'r reading *Black Friday*, from th *Cherub* series.

Maisie, age

I often get told off for reading when I should be doing my homework! I have loved to read for as long as I can remember. We always read a book as a family on holidays and my dad sometimes makes up stories. My dad randomly buys me new books. I'm reading *Hunger* by Michael Grant.

Cheryl, age 13

I got into reading by reading short fan fiction about One Direction. As the days passed I started reading other books.

Berivan, age 14

I read books that look interesting. Once I get into the book I can't get my head out of it. Then I either read sequels or similar books.

Kellie, age 14

When I was little my parents took me to the library. Ever since then I have had a reading habit.

Kajoul, age 14

I love reading and read everything everywhere. I do my homework quickly and to a good quality so that I can read. I got the habit because my mum read to me when I was little and she also wanted me to read to her. We have no screen time on weekdays except TV at dinner. My dad used to read the newspaper to me. Sometimes they still read to me now, especially near to Christmas. Sometimes I ask to be read to at other times.

Shannon, age 13

BOYS

I love reading book[s] by authors I like an[d] books based on vide[o] games I play.

Nat, age 1[?]

I don't really make time for reading. I just read when I don't have much to do. I read when I am bored and if it is good I carry on. I'm reading *The Short Second Life of Bree Tanner*.

Sam, age 12

I have always been in the habit of reading when I need a break, instead of going on electronic devices. I am allowed three hours of screen time a week. I'm reading *Young Bond*.

Oliver, age 12

I got my reading habit from reading books that tell me new things. Also from reading interesting books like *To Kill a Mockingbird* and *Of Mice and Men*. *Skulduggery Pleasant* is a favourite of mine.

Zinadin, age 15

I read in my room in the afternoon and evening. I am only allowed my electronic devices on the weekend.

Kai, age 14

I feel good about reading. I sort of have a reading habit; it came from holidays with no internet signal or TV. It sparks my imagination. I'm reading *The Great Gatsby* at the moment.

Joe, age 13

I'd rather do something outdoors than read a book for enjoyment. I really only read when I am bored. I read the newspaper my dad brings home from work and I ask my dad for ideas on what to read or I find something that is popular.

Ossy, age 13

I don't like most books so I read magazines about football and gaming, and newspapers.

Toby, age 12

Limit screen time

You need to help your child by making space for reading. With busy lives and devices at a child's fingertips, seemingly filling up every available moment, it's important to create some balance by carving out quiet time at home for reading. As before, it follows that screen time should be restricted. Free reign with screen time is not good for teens as they will not self-regulate. You need to have rules and stick to them. This might not be easy! Remember your teen will be inclined to do the opposite of what you say at some point, and it can be difficult to stick to your guns. It helps your resolve, I think, if you ask yourself one of life's big questions, 'What do I really want for my child?' If you want them to spend time on things other than screen time, you need to take action.

> **EXPERT VIEW**
>
> Consistency is really important and the goal is to help children learn to self-regulate, so build up trust and explain how they will get more freedom and choice if they comply with certain rules. Reducing conflict generally will, in turn, promote reading as the atmosphere will be less stressful and your teen won't be inclined to deliberately go against your wishes.
>
> *Dr Amanda Gummer*

Of course I'm not saying you should say an outright 'no' to screens – technology brings so many opportunities and benefits to us all – but limiting time spent on them is a good strategy. For instance, we have a house rule that says no gaming from ꞏnday to Thursday, and we impose a time limit on ꞏy, Saturday and Sunday. However, any gaming is only ꞏd after homework is completed.

According to research carried out by Childwise, teens would miss their phones above any other device. A separate report by Ofcom shows that the number of texts sent by 12–15 year olds grew from an average of 104 per week in 2009 to 255 per week in 2013. There are no indications that this growth will slow down.

No technology in bedrooms is the ideal. To be honest, this is easier to enforce when they are younger. So if you want to introduce new rules in the teen years, for instance, if they have had a TV in their room for ages and you want to make a new start, it is going to be hard to remove it. But that's not to say that you shouldn't do it. You can say no to things! The earlier in the teenage years that you set the house rules the better, and the easier it will be for a child to accept. Think about what could happen if you don't! I spoke to a 13 year old girl who told me that if she can't sleep at night she winds down by playing *Mario Bros* in bed on her DS. In such a situation, reading a book really doesn't stand a chance!

(For more information about screen time see pages 18–31.)

Be flexible

Your approach to parenting needs to change as the years go by, and with teens you need to be both firm and flexible. For instance, most teens seem to be almost surgically attached to their phone – it's how they keep in touch with their friends, after all. And because teens tend to hang out in their rooms a lot, it becomes more difficult to prevent them having phones in their bedroom. So they may be texting and using social networks when you don't want them to. Just how realistic is it to expect and hope for them to read if they have their phone at their fingertip

A good compromise may be that at bedtime, when it is reading time (and sleeping time!), the phone leaves the bedroom and is put on charge somewhere else until the morning. Rules like this are more palatable if they are family rules. Because I and my husband don't have phones in the bedroom either it's an easy rule for my son to accept. You need to find rules that will work for your family – every family is different.

> My daughter won't read. I have read to her over the years and have always had books in the house. Now she only wants to be on the phone or the laptop. She spends ages in her bedroom watching TV and texting. How do I confiscate a phone from a 15 year old?
>
> *Mum to Scarlet, age 15*

📖 Encourage the habit

Don't put pressure on your teen or nag them to read more, this strategy will probably backfire. Teens commonly do go through phases of not being that interested in reading, just like adults do. It's easy to feel anxious as a parent, to feel that they should be reading all the time, every day, because you are so conscious of how important reading is. But try to relax because it will ebb and flow. Don't worry about it, just continue to encourage them with a light touch and keep the big picture in your head. Getting a reading habit is a marathon, not a sprint!

Realistically, with such busy school lives and an increasingly independent social life, bedtime is the most logical and perhaps most beneficial time to read. Talk to them about how reading at bedtime can help them relax and unwind. Other reading opportunities are the journey to and from school, weekends, after school when homework is done, and in the holidays.

You could also consider talking to your teen about the importance of reading in the bigger picture. You can tell them how reading will help them in their life, how they will find success at school and in the workplace, and how it will open up different life experiences for them. It will make them feel more grown up that you are able to talk to them as an equal about this.

If reading to relax does not appeal to them, then there are other benefits you can hook them in with – perhaps something more immediate and tangible. For instance, by reading they can become expert on anything they are interested in – pop music, horses, cartoons, nature, cooking, astronomy.... They can also read about other teenagers and their lives and problems and use the experiences they read about to help them with the difficult things they encounter.

<table>
<tr><td>EXPERT VIEW</td><td>It is important to make the connections between other aspects of the life of your teenager and reading. Popular culture, particularly film and television, but also music, can be at the centre of a constellation of sources of reading pleasure. A popular film may be based on a novel, or may give rise to the book of the film, plus there will be a website, and possibly a game or an app. Well-known music groups generally have books, particularly biographies, written about them which will be devoured by teenage readers. Current favourites at the time of writing are films of *The Hunger Games* and the group One Direction, which have both enjoyed enormous spin-off book sales and prompted a huge amount of reading.

David Reedy</td></tr>
</table>

📖 Treat any reading as 'normal'

I suggest that when they do read you shouldn't make a big deal of it! Often, if they think there is something you really want them to do, they will do the complete opposite to be contrary, assert independence and show you that they don't have to do what you want. Treat any reading as completely normal. After all, this is what the goal is: reading for pleasure should become second nature. When children read and enjoy the experience, the reading itself becomes the reward.

📖 Regular reading time is still the ideal

Your teen's habit may be to read daily, several times a week, or less frequently than that (perhaps every weekend), but it can still be a regular habit. Regular is what you need ideally, because this is of course how habits get embedded. If your teen is busy in the week and still does not like to read at bedtime, but sits down every weekend to read, and really looks forward to it, then you have a really positive situation.

As I've said before, the reading habit is something that is gained over time. Don't force it, but always encourage reading in any way you can. And always set a good example yourself. That way you will provide a positive role model for your child even if, as a teenager, they will probably scoff at it!

How to read

I have found through my research that lots of parents don't consider they need to, or indeed can, play an active role in encouraging reading with their teens. Some don't think they could make a difference, some simply don't think their encouragement or involvement is necessary.

You absolutely can make a difference and you are needed! Your level of involvement with your teen's reading can range from very close and 'hands on' (if you co-read for instance – see pages 102–3) to more of a sharing and chatting relationship. Indeed, as your child grows up, it's natural to move to a more reciprocal relationship with reading. As their reading material becomes more sophisticated you can share books, recommend titles to each other and discuss what you have read.

• **Be sensitive to their need** to be seen as grown up and an individual with their own valid views. Never criticise or belittle their reading choices. Listen to their opinions and have friendly relaxed conversations. As you chat about books or magazines, the conversation may well move to other things and this is a great example of what I mean about reading being relationship glue. It becomes an enabler for closeness. Your child should feel able to confide in you and this will help them with the myriad challenges they face.

For many reluctant readers, the only books they are likely to read are the ones they have to for English at school. The danger is, of course, that these books will automatically be seen as boring because they are homework. You can try helping in several ways.

• **You can suggest that you co-read** the book if they are finding it hard-going, and so try to make it enjoyable. This may work best for younger teens. Or you could read it yourself separately, so that you can chat about it. But make sure you don't come across as if you are checking up on your teen – instead, show how much you want to read it for yourself and are interested. Or you could say 'It's been years since I read that, I'd love to re-read it', or 'I've never read that but always wanted to'.

Some teens will like your interest; some will hate it! Again, you know your child, and you know if this strategy is a good one for you or not. An added benefit of knowing the book they are studying is that you can help them with any English homework by acting as a sounding board for their ideas. One mum recounted how her son, Ollie, age 14, moaned like mad about having to read *The Hound of the Baskervilles* by Arthur Conan Doyle, telling her 'It's rubbish, it's so boring.' However, after she put on a DVD of the *Sherlock* TV series he took more interest in it.

> **EXPERT VIEW**
>
> Most books now read in English lessons have a film made about them. So it's well worth getting them in as DVDs to help promote the interest.
>
> *David Reedy*

• **Swap books and recommend books** to your teen. If they recommend one to you, make sure you read it! Embrace the chance to share. Enjoy the new dynamic of having a fellow reader in the home with whom you can share the fun. Enjoy chatting about what you read.

One mother told me that her son completely stopped reading at the age of 14 having previously been a voracious and enthusiastic reader. He simply switched off and started playing computer games, having shown no interest in them before. Their relationship suffered hugely. She and her partner could find nothing to talk to him about positively and all the communication resulted in conflict. The mother and her partner despaired. But suddenly, at the age of 17, he got his reading habit back and started recommending books for her to read. And she reciprocated. He hasn't stopped gaming, but there is a balance now and they have something positive and creative to talk about and bond over.

• **Try going to book events** together if you can. This has several benefits: you are sharing the enjoyment together, you are getting inspiration for what to read, and you are seeing other teens there who are into reading.

When you go shopping together, make a point of always going into a bookshop and perhaps treating yourselves to a new book each. This is a great way to give a child independence of choice. Browse the shelves and let your teen go and look at whatever they want to. As lots of bookshops have cafés now, why not have a coffee together too and expand the enjoyment of the whole experience. You could also try sharing books that have been made into films and watch the film together as well.

• **Set an example** and show you enjoy reading because this is still very important. Try to think of new ways to share reading. A mum of two boys, ages 14 and 12, told me they have a new family routine at weekends when they all snuggle up on the bed together, mum in the middle, each with their own book, and they read. It's a special family time and the mum is giving a strong message that reading is a great way to spend free time, reinforcing the idea that reading is a pleasure.

Rose, age 14, visits her 89 year old gran every Saturday afternoon. She sits with her and has tea and chats, and every time her gran reads aloud to her. While listening, Rose may draw or even knit. But mostly she just listens, wrapped up in her gran's tartan blanket, while her gran works through her old copies of classics such as *The Railway Children*. Rose loves this and looks forward to it every week.

• **If you have built up a co-reading habit** over the recent years you have an amazing opportunity now to continue – well into their teens if possible. Grab it! The longer you can keep it going (whether on a daily or less frequent basis) the better.

As each month and year goes by, you are embedding the habit and love for reading more firmly. And if you are still reading to your teen, keep on going. I know of teens who routinely have two books on the go, one they read themselves and one they co-read. The girls from one family I met like to read independently but enjoy being read to as well:

> My daughter, 13, has her 'private books' – Sophie Kinsella and such-like – teen books. We read and share other books, mostly ones she wouldn't really read on her own. *The Little Grey Men* is a family favourite. We all love it: Jasmine, Kelly and me. Even their dad listens to me reading sometimes, when he is home in time.
>
> *Mum of Jasmine, age 13, and Kelly, age 8*

By giving them your time, you are showing them clearly that you value and love them. They need to know this in order for them to navigate the challenges they face.

EXPERT VIEW

Various research has shown that healthy attachment is vital for future emotional health, and teens who are securely attached are able to cope with increasing independence as they know they have a secure anchor to return to when necessary.

Dr Amanda Gummer

Sadly, as children grow and become more mature, physical contact becomes less easy and less frequent. Reading offers a way of being physically close in a comfortable, easy and natural way. The relationship glue I talked about is very powerful when you get time together, are able to give attention to your teen and both enjoy co-reading. (For a lovely description of this, see the Rob and Ella quote on page 151.)

• **As they grow up**, things will change and your time reading together will be reduced. Your teen will eventually not want to share reading any more, but certainly in the early teen years you should be able to keep it going. From families I have talked with who have kept it up, it's clear that reading together is just what they do, as normal as brushing teeth before bedtime, and so not a big deal at all. And teens love to be read to just as much as anyone else! You might be surprised how long your child is happy to continue.

I mentioned in the last chapter that there is a prevalent view that reading to your child is babyish, and that independent reading is some kind of yardstick to measure their maturity by. This is nonsense, and if you don't think reading aloud is babyish, they will be much less likely to think that too. Granted, they may not want to tell their friends about it, but that's fine. It can be a private family thing.

• **As your child gets older** and becomes more physically self-conscious with you, you may want to change your location when reading. For instance, in the past your child may have been very happy snuggling up in bed while you read, but at some point along the way this might begin to feel awkward. Be sensitive to your teen. You can still do bedtime reading – try sitting on the bed, or bring a chair into bedroom. Find a way that works for you and your child.

One mum I know sits on the sofa with her 15 year old son every evening – he throws his legs over her and she reads aloud, then he takes his turn – it's comfortable physical contact for them both. And the mum also greatly enjoys being read to. Another strategy is to try co-reading at weekends. While it may seem strange or impossible to think of reading at bedtime every day to a 16 year old, weekend co-reading sessions on a Sunday afternoon, say, curled up on the sofa with tea and cake, can seem very acceptable!

If you have already stopped co-reading you might ask them if they'd like to start again. Give it a go – they may say yes. It certainly shouldn't be something that is imposed, like doing household chores, so it doesn't have to be every night, maybe just at weekends, or holidays, or just from time to time.

> Reading to my own children was always the highlight of my day and I made time at least three times a week to do so. In fact I read to my son until, at age 12, he turned to me and asked if it was about time I stopped. I agreed to read him only one more story and took *Lord of the Rings* off the shelf!
>
> *David Reedy*

• **When your children are out of the home** a lot, when time is short, when they have a social life and seem to just drop in for meals before rushing out again, you may find that it helps to actually schedule time together. This strategy will really show them how you think reading and being together is important, so important you want to make sure there is time for it in your diary!

What to read

Aside from the challenge of making time, a place and a routine for reading, not being able to find anything to read is one of the biggest complaints of teenagers. Your help is needed!

		Age 8–11 (school years 3, 4, 5, 6)	Age 12–14 (school years 7, 8, 9)	Age 15–16 (school years 10, 11)
I cannot find things to read that interest me	Boys	28%	38%	43%
	Girls	22%	30%	33%

National Literacy Trust, 2013 survey

📖 Pick up on anything that interests them

As with any other age, be constantly on the lookout for opportunities to connect reading with what they are into and what is popular. For example, if they love a TV series and there is also a book, give them the book to read. Films can be a huge motivation for reading books. If they have seen a film they loved and there is a book, give it to them and tell them books always have more in them than the films, so it will be even better! Good examples here are *The Hunger Games*, *The Hobbit*, *The Lord of the Rings*, *The Perks of Being a Wallflower*, the *Twilight* series and so many more. If they are mad about celebs, give them biographies about their favourites. There is a book or magazine for every possible interest – cookery books, manga, graphic novels, adventure, romance, fantasy! Everyone loves a good laugh – try books about their favourite comedian, or books with humorous observations, such as those by Bill Bryson. Sports mad? How about a biography about their sports hero, or hand them the sports pages of your daily newspaper. If they love fashion, there are plenty of books about that, from *The Devil Wears Prada* or a biography about Coco Chanel to encyclopedias about the history of fashion.

As with younger years, getting into a series is always a good idea for the obvious reason that the next book is ready and waiting. Similarly, if they have enjoyed a book by an author, look for another by the same person. Encourage your child to go to the local or school library and ask there for new books. Suggest they ask their friends. Even better, ask their friends yourself! When their friends visit, strike up a conversation about reading, telling them what you are reading, and asking them what they have enjoyed recently. This is a great way to normalise reading, and you become an enabler for a conversation about it. I have had some amazing chats about books with my son and his friends by starting the conversation myself.

> **EXPERT VIEW**
>
> Peer group is so important at this age. If you know any of their friends who are readers, encourage swapping and ask them what they are reading – it's sometimes easier for teens to talk with their friends' parents than with their own!
>
> *David Reedy*

Magazines are an obvious choice here too. In fact, magazines can be a great help in overcoming a reading hiatus. They are often very interesting to teens, with their appealing 'dip in and out' content, making them feel connected to their popular culture.

If your teen is fascinated by gadgets, you may find e-reading is a novelty and a hook. Indeed, if they go to college or university, e-readers and tablets can be a great way to avoid carrying around a lot of very heavy reference books. Other kinds of digital reading include reading straight off the web. There is a lot of original writing to be found on sites such as Wattpad. Many teens get into this, and there is plenty of teen fiction, much of it written by teens themselves. These sites offer interaction where teens can post comments and reviews about what they have read.

I know it is easy to feel anxious about digital reading because you can't readily see what it is your child is reading and know if it's appropriate. But you can always ask them what the story is and chat about it. Try not to worry. All reading is good reading! It shows they are interested in reading for pleasure. If your teen's attention is captured, view it as an opportunity to build on further and encourage wider reading.

EXPERT VIEW

Reading on sites such as Wattpad is good in two ways. Not only are teenagers reading, but they are encouraged to write because they see what other teenagers have written and had published on the site.

David Reedy

I started reading on the internet. I rather like to read on the internet as I think there is more variety when choosing, in comparison with physical books. I started slowly after we got home broadband and started getting into Wikipedia. I started researching computing which also improved my English and my knowledge about technology and IT.

Umut, age 14

📖 Anything goes!

Keep in mind that your teen needs to feel individual, to see themselves as separate from you, with their own views. So they need to make their own choices about what to read. Striking a balance here can be tricky. You need to help and encourage without pushing or overwhelming. The answer is to suggest plenty of things without forcing your opinion on them; give them the chance to make their own selection. You might long for them to read the classics, for example, as you did, but if *Wimpy Kid* keeps on appearing, or their nose is buried in magazines, do not give out disapproving messages. The most important thing is that your teen is enjoying reading.

Really it's just the same as with younger years. You need to expose your teen to a variety of different reading material. They are working out their identity, exploring what kind of a person they are, what they are interested in. Trying different books is like trying on identities – 'Am I a thrillers kind of guy?', 'Do I enjoy traditional romance or vampire books?' and so on. So keep on showing them new and different things, really whatever you can lay your hands on, but don't add pressure; read yourself at any visible opportunity; and DON'T NAG, as this can backfire horribly: Sam, age 15, told me: 'Everyone keeps on at me to read – mum, dad, my teachers, even granny. It just annoys me.'

📖 Reading doesn't always mean finishing

It's perfectly fine for them to start reading something and then think 'This is not for me,' and stop! Make sure your teen realises they don't have to finish something if it doesn't click. The more books they read, the more it will help them work out their likes and dislikes and reflect their growing sense of individuality.

📖 Try to make sure it's not too advanced

You may sometimes want to say no to reading matter, although clearly if you prohibit reading material you may make it all the more appealing. If your child seems to be reading something you are really concerned about, that seems wholly inappropriate, read it yourself so that you have a balanced and informed view. Then explain to her why you don't like it. I did talk with a mum whose 12 year old daughter asked her if she could read *50 Shades of Grey*. The mum said 'no' and explained why. Of course it's hard to police completely and that girl may still read the book with her friends. The best thing about that example is, I think, that the girl asked her mum if she could read it – the conversation was easy between them because they are used to chatting about books, and so the mum was able to put her view across.

> **EXPERT VIEW**
>
> Being open to discussing the content of books that a child has come across, even if you're not happy that he/she's read them will enable you to maintain easy dialogue with your child about reading. Your child will feel safe reading new and challenging material as they'll have the reassurance that they can talk to you about anything they don't understand.
>
> *Dr Amanda Gummer*

It is very likely your child will still go through phases of not wanting to read anything too challenging. This is fine. You probably go through phases like that yourself, I know I do. They may also go through phases of not feeling like reading at all. Be patient – all things change with time and it does not mean your child has become a non-reader. Something will hook them back in – perhaps something completely different. One dad told me:

> My son seemed to have a dip in enthusiasm and reverted from reading quite challenging books to reading his manga books. He is very visual – he loves to draw and really enjoys illustrations, so I searched online for some interesting graphic novels and found Hunt Emerson's comic books [of classic titles] and bought a couple. I left them on the chair in the sitting room. Of course he picked them up and seemed quite interested. I said that I thought he might like them. At bedtime he said, Dad, I'm not going to read *Naruto* tonight, I'm going to read *Dante's Inferno* instead!
>
> *Alan, dad to Lucas, age 13*

The Reading Home

Having all sorts of reading material in every room continues to be important. In particular, teens tend to spend a long time in the bedroom, so make sure they have a well-stocked bookshelf and magazines to hand. You want them to pick up reading material as well as technology. One family I visited recently had a range of books in the bathroom, from poetry anthologies to a book about different toilets in the world, to Greek mythology, to fiction. Bathtime is reading time in their home and their children routinely read while relaxing in the bath.

You need to have rules about screen time, create quiet time where reading can happen, and make reading very visible. You need to set an example, both with reading for pleasure and with making sure you have time offline. Talk about books and share books. Give them as gifts and show they are desirable and valuable. If you can, enlist other role models such as a cool aunt or uncle, or a friend of the family they look up to, to talk about their favourite books or magazines. And be gender neutral – don't ever give any credence to the pervading belief that boys and reading don't mix. They can and do!

Dos and Don'ts

Dos

✓ Stay involved with your teen's reading – in the most appropriate way you can. Recognise your reading relationship will evolve as they mature.

✓ Continue to read to and with your teen as long as you can, well into the teenage years if possible.

✓ Share and recommend books, making your home a place where reading and books are talked about.

✓ If your teen recommends a book to you, or an article, make sure you read it and talk about afterwards – respect their reading choices.

✓ Set an example and read in front of them.

✓ Have rules about screen time – both for you and your child – and stick to them.

✓ Have a rule about no technology (especially no phones) in the bedroom at night.

✓ Have a wide range of reading material available – all kinds of books and magazines and newspapers.

✓ Help them find things they want to read by looking out for books and magazines and articles that reflect their interests and passions.

✓ Encourage them to choose their own reading material independently.

✓ Share reading in a wider way by going to events together, and make a trip to the bookshop a regular part of your shopping outings.

✓ Keep the big picture in mind; acquiring a lifelong reading habit is a marathon, not a sprint.

✓ Keep gently encouraging your teen and avoid pressuring them.

Dont's

✘ Don't put your teen under pressure to read. Encourage but don't nag.

✘ Don't interfere too much – try to strike a balance of maintaining involvement and encouragement and keeping a good supply of reading material available, while allowing them to be themselves and make their own reading choices.

✘ Don't ever give any credence to the pervading view that girls are more likely to read than boys.

✘ Don't criticise their reading choice or show any disapproval. If something seems really inappropriate, read it yourself so that you have a valid view and explain why you don't like it.

✘ Don't make too much fuss and 'hang out the flags' if they are reading.

Q &A

My teen says there is nothing interesting to read. Everything I suggest is 'boring'. How do I make headway?

Don't give up – there truly is something to interest everyone. Think hard around what they do like. For instance, if he only wants to play *Call of Duty* then buy him a strategy guide. Only interested in make-up? Buy her a book about how to apply it and create new looks. Once they have read something and enjoyed it, follow up with something else. Strike while the iron's hot!

When I try to introduce new rules about screen time and technology there are huge screaming rows. How can I make her listen? I wonder if it is all worth it.

First of all, don't give in. Remember who is in charge – it's you! It's your home and you make the rules. Explain that you are not saying no to all screen time, just setting out the rules of engagement. You might have to accept the family upsets as a short-term unpleasantness, but remember your bigger goal. If you want to help her love reading, she needs time to be able to read!

Nothing I say is right. If I try to talk to him about reading he just switches off. How can I get him to listen?

Don't take it personally! If your direct approach is not working, try being indirect and make it easier for your teen. Choose books for him from time to time and simply leave them on his bedside table so that he can look at them without feeling watched. Don't make a song and dance about it. Or enlist the help of a cool uncle or family friend to talk about books they like or give books at birthdays and Christmas.

Our daughter used to read every day but now she shows very little interest. How can we get her back into it?

Don't put pressure on her. It's fairly common for reading to take a bit of a dip at some stage in the teenage years. There is so much else taking up their attention. Accept it is less frequent, but gently try to keep it ticking over. Different types of reading material might click better, magazines, books about popular culture. Try not to worry, she should come back to it in the end.

Developmental stages

These are key developmental areas for 12–16 year olds.

SOCIAL AND EMOTIONAL SKILLS
- Friends will become more important than parents in influencing interests.
- Will become increasingly emotionally independent from parents.
- Want to express their own individuality more.
- Communication is increasingly digital.
- Self-esteem is vulnerable while the sense of self is maturing and teens can seem overly sensitive to negative thoughts about themselves.

THINKING SKILLS
- Teens will be developing complex thought patterns and be capable of dealing with abstract and hypothetical concepts.

PHYSICAL DEVELOPMENT
- Hormones will be volatile and teens' moods may fluctuate wildly within short periods of time.
- Puberty brings a vast array of physical changes but social and thinking skills don't necessarily all develop at the same rate.

NOTE TO PARENTS: the speed of child development varies hugely from child to child and different skills are mastered at different ages – often determined by a child's environment. However, whatever age they acquire these skills, they are acquired in sequence, so children build up more complex skills on the foundations of previously mastered simpler skills. For example, a child cannot learn to write using fine motor skills until he or she has mastered the gross motor skills that underpin the muscle development. Above all, remember no two children are the same!

Father and daughter (age 17) talk about reading together.

Rob says:

My daughter, Ella, has never been a great reader, much to my disappointment. My wife and I did what lots of parents do and stopped reading to her at about 10 years old, thinking she would carry on independently. Ella is now 17. I heard about the benefits of reading to your child well into their teens and decided to give it a go, even though she is actually almost out of her teens! I have a very busy job and travel a lot so getting time together with my children is not always easy, but I suggested to her that we might try reading together again and to my real surprise she was keen!

We did it for about three months and it was a lovely experience. I got to be close to my daughter, we read books together, taking it in turns to read aloud to each other, cuddling up in the armchair. It gave me a connection with my teen daughter. She is often out and about with her extensive social life. My time with her is limited and I find the time I do have with her tends to be very practical e.g. when will you pick me up or can I have £20. Reading together gave me a glimpse of the daughter I remember as a child. The physical proximity from reading together was great. It can be awkward at this age — for instance I tend to get side-on hugs now. Reading allowed us to be physically close without any self-consciousness. Diarising time to read together felt really good, to consciously make time for each other.

I am disappointed I could not carry on — my work schedule prevented it — but the really interesting thing is Ella is now reading more on her own, and is talking to me about the books she reads. It really did bring us closer and ignited a renewed interest in reading for her.

Ella says:

I really enjoyed reading with my dad; it was good to spend quality time with him. It made books more interesting hearing different voices read the words. I don't normally read a lot and it made it fun and more enjoyable for me.

Bookshelf

Here is a list of all the books that have been mentioned. I've sorted them into approximate stages, but remember these are just an indication. That's why some of the books appear in more than one stage. I hope they give you some ideas and inspiration. If your child seems ready to read more challenging books that is great, or if, for instance, your child has just started school and still wants something like *The Tiger Who Came to Tea*, it's really no problem at all. The thing is to keep reading!

Pre-school

Cats Ahoy!, Peter Bently and Jim Field
Dave and the Tooth Fairy, Verna Allette Wilkins and Paul Hunt
Dear Zoo, Rod Campbell
Dogger, Shirley Hughes
Elmer, David McKee
Hubert Horatio Bartle Bobton-Trent, Lauren Child
Jump Up and Join In series, Carrie and David Grant
Lucy & Tom at the Seaside, Shirley Hughes
Maisy series, Lucy Cousins
Mrs Nibble Moves House, Jane Pilgrim
My Big Shouting Day!, Rebecca Patterson
The Complete Book of First Experiences, Anne Civardi and Stephen Cartwright
The Giant Jam Sandwich, John Vernon Lord and Janet Burroway
The House at Pooh Corner, A. A. Milne
The Jolly Postman, Janet and Allan Ahlberg
The Snail and the Whale, Julia Donaldson and Axel Scheffler
The Tale of the Flopsy Bunnies, Beatrix Potter
The Tiger Who Came to Tea, Judith Kerr
The Very Hungry Caterpillar, Eric Carle
Topsy and Tim series, Jean and Gareth Adamson
Where's Spot?, Eric Hill

Character brands
Ben 10
Fireman Sam
Mr Men and Little Miss
Peppa Pig
Thomas the Tank Engine

Starting school

Amelia Jane series, Enid Blyton
Artemis Fowl series, Eoin Colfer
Asterix series, René Goscinny and Albert Uderzo
Cops and Robbers, Janet and Allan Ahlberg
Hammy the Wonder Hamster, Poppy Harris
Horrid Henry series, Francesca Simon
Mr Wolf's Pancakes, Jan Fearnley
Mummy Laid an Egg!, Babette Cole
My Naughty Little Sister Collection, Dorothy Edwards and
    Shirley Hughes
Paddle-to-the-Sea, Holling Clancy Holling
Secret Agent Jack Stalwart: the Search for the Sunken Treasure: Australia,
    Elizabeth Singer Hunt
Shouty Arthur, Angie Morgan
The Most Impossible Parents, Brian Patten
Tintin series, Georges Remi Hergé
Topsy and Tim Have Itchy Heads, Jean and Gareth Adamson
Wilf Weasel's Speedy Skates, Edward Holmes

Non-fiction

Chameleons Are Cool, Martin Jenkins and Sue Shields
Fly Traps! Plants that bite back, Martin Jenkins and David Parkins
In One End and Out the Other, Mike Goldsmith and Richard Watson
Is a Big Blue Whale the Biggest Thing There Is?, Robert E. Wells
Logic Puzzles, Sarah Khan
Read and Wonder series
See Inside series
Think of an Eel, Karen Wallace and Mike Bostock

Poetry

Noisy Poems, Jill Bennett and Nick Sharratt
Revolting Rhymes, Roald Dahl
Silly Verse for Kids, Spike Milligan

Choosing to read

Alex Rider series, Anthony Horowitz
Alice's Adventures in Wonderland and Through the Looking-Glass,
    Lewis Carroll
Artemis Fowl series, Eoin Colfer
Asterix series, René Goscinny and Albert Uderzo
Ballet Shoes, Noel Streatfeild
Coming to England, Floella Benjamin

Dante's Inferno comic book, Hunt Emerson
Diary of a Wimpy Kid series, Jeff Kinney
Dork Diaries series, Rachel Renée Russell
Football Academy series, Tom Palmer
Grandpa Chatterji, Jamila Gavin
Harry Potter series, J. K. Rowling
Mary Poppins, P. L. Travers
My Family and Other Animals, Gerald Durrell
Stig of the Dump, Clive King
Swallows and Amazons, Arthur Ransome
The Arrival, Shaun Tan
The Little Grey Men, B.B.
Tintin series, Georges Remi Hergé
Tom's Midnight Garden, Philippa Pearce
Tracy Beaker series, Jacqueline Wilson
Varjak Paw, S. F. Said
War Horse, Michael Morpurgo
Young Samurai series, Chris Bradford
You're a Bad Man, Mr Gum!, Andy Stanton

Poetry
A Shame To Miss, Anne Fine
All the Best: The Selected Poems of Roger McGough
Cautionary Verses, Hilaire Belloc
'Cargoes' by John Masefield and 'Night Mail' by W. H. Auden, in *I Like This Poem: A Collection of Best-loved Poems Chosen by Children for Other Children*
Jabberwocky and Other Poems, Lewis Carroll
Old Possum's Book of Practical Cats, T. S. Eliot
Orange Silver Sausage, compiled by James Carter and Graham Denton
Silly Verse for Kids, Spike Milligan
The Complete Nonsense of Edward Lear

Non-fiction
Maps, Aleksandra and Daniel Mizielinski
Mummies: Mysteries of the Ancient World, Paul Harrison
Stitch-by-Stitch, Jane Bull
The Football Book

Character brands
Minecraft
Moshi Monsters
Skylanders

Staying connected
Alex Rider series, Anthony Horowitz
Black Friday, Cherub series, Robert Muchamore
Hunger, Gone series, Michael Grant
My Family and Other Animals, Gerald Durrell
Naruto series, Masashi Kishimoto
Noughts and Crosses series, Malorie Blackman
Of Mice and Men, John Steinbeck
Skulduggery Pleasant series, Derek Landy
The Curious Incident of the Dog in the Night-time, Mark Haddon
The Devil Wears Prada, Lauren Weisberger
The Great Gatsby, F. Scott Fitzgerald
The Greengage Summer, Rumer Godden
The Hobbit, J. R. R. Tolkien
The Hound of the Baskervilles, Arthur Conan Doyle
The Hunger Games, Suzanne Collins
The L-Shaped Room, Lynne Reid Banks
The Little Grey Men, B. B.
The Lord of the Rings, J. R. R. Tolkien
The Perks of Being a Wallflower, Stephen Chbosky
The Railway Children, E. Nesbit
The Secret Dreamworld of a Shopaholic, Sophie Kinsella
The Short Second Life of Bree Tanner, Stephenie Meyer
To Kill a Mockingbird, Harper Lee
Twilight series, Stephenie Meyer
Young Bond series, Charlie Higson

Non-fiction
Call of Duty: Ghosts Strategy Guide
Notes from a Small Island, Bill Bryson
Dare to Dream: Life as One Direction
Stitch-by-Stitch, Jane Bull
The Football Book
The Little Book of Chanel, Emma Baxter-Wright
Txtng: The Gr8 Db8, David Crystal

Resources

If you want to read a bit more around the subject, you might find the following interesting:

Aric Sigman: www.aricsigman.com

Booktrust's book finder: www.booktrust.org.uk

Love reading for kids: www.lovereading4kids.co.uk

National Literacy Trust: www.literacytrust.org.uk

Ofcom media and communications reports: www.ofcom.org.uk

Proust and the Squid: The Story and Science of the Reading Brain, Maryanne Wolf

The Reading Promise, Alice Ozma

The UK Literacy Association: www.ukla.org

Thanks to

Dr Amanda Gummer, David Reedy and Dr Aric Sigman for their advice and comments; the pupils, parents and staff at Wendell Park School, Shepherd's Bush, London W12, the pupils and staff at Woodside High School, Wood Green, London N22, and Twyford C of E High School, Acton, London W3; all the many parents and children I have talked with – thank you for sharing your feelings so candidly; Rebecca Ironside and the team at SPA Future Thinking; Reeta Bhatiani, Cally Poplak and Rob McMenemy for all their support; and last, but not least, Martin and Miranda – I couldn't have done it without you!